Cleveland City Guide 2020

by Valentine Reedy
edited by Linda Reedy

ISBN: 978-1-877912-61-0

Going to Cleveland? In Cleveland? Into Cleveland?

Cleveland City Guide 2020 is a city guide to Cleveland that gets you off on the right foot: Especially if you are walking, biking, or using Cleveland's outstanding public transit. Cleveland 2020 City Guide was created just that way. Our travel content creators walked, took trains, buses, and rode bikes to put this easy-to-use book together. So almost all of the places 0mentioned in Cleveland 2020 City Guide are easily accessible without a car. it is also a great way to see Cleveland and save money at the same time.

This city guide is about the core area of Cleveland starting in Downtown Cleveland and heading east to University Circle and Little Italy, and then to the west side neighborhoods of Tremont, Ohio City, and Gordon Square. With Lakewood included, to boot.

Most of all you will see that we had a blast making Cleveland City Guide 2020. That is what we want to share with you. Cleveland City Guide 2020 will give you a great start to a superb visit to Cleveland in 2020. Enjoy.

About the Reedys:

Val and Linda are a travel/city guide dynamic duo. Val and Linda love to travel, and have made the so-called Rust Belt cities of the Upper Midwest (they like to call them the Great Lake Cities – so no more negative Rust Belt talk – please) their metier.

Being an active couple, they swear by seeing a city on foot, on bikes, and by using public transportation. As they say, ". . .moving around any city in a car is like being in a metal and glass cocoon. Once you get away from them, it's all butterflies."

Val and Linda love to read your comments and ideas. The best way to do that is, of course, leave a review. And, if you want more direct contact please go to the Cardinal Content website:

https://cardinalcontentebook.weebly.com/

Table of Contents:

Cleveland, Ohio

When we published our latest series of City/Travel Guides in Cleveland beginning back in 2013 we were still disposed to consider Cleveland as the Rust Belt City that was on the rise, though much was, perhaps, lacking. Not now. Cleveland is simply the Rust Belt City, the Largest City in Ohio, the City of the Upper Midwest and Northeastern US that is fullfilling its promise of renewal and 21st Century change and possibilities. Nothing is teetering, or lackluster about Cleveland's comeback. It is an certain as the Cavalier's recent Championship season, though we dare say some Clevelanders may yet pinch themselves to make sure they did not dream up that NBA Dream Season.

And it is with abundant price that we are publishing anew this Cleveland 2018 City Guide both an ebook and a Print On Demand paperback. So many changes have occurred over just the last few years that this series deserves to be restarted with an up-to-date perpective and point-of-view.

So, let us first start where we were back in 2013. Then we were enthusiastic, and realistic:

With Cleveland you get a lot of what you expect, and even more of what you do not expect. What you may expect is a weathered, tough as nails Midwest/Eastern City with a diverse population, economic challenges, fascinating history, and a better future just already in view. You may think rough winters, sudden springs, long hot summers, baleful autumns, and then the polar reaches come back for a long and not always welcomed visit.

Each season comes with sublime events and traditions. Some are as ancient as the Great Lake Erie and its inland marine environment. Others are only as old as a year ago. Some are tied to the American scene; some are part of the religious year's calendar, and still others are just good time for good time's sake. Indeed, if there is anything that is absolutely true about Cleveland it is its unabashed ability to have a good time. Even if Rock n Roll is not the Lingua Franca of popular music it may have been, the verve and exuberance that are its hallmarks are evident each time Cleveland and Clevelanders have a party.

Cleveland is a town so dedicated to the vigorous enjoyment of life that it leaves no real room for self-consciousness exclusivity. The only criterion it seems to having a good time in Cleveland is a willingness to do so with energy, passion, and a decent level of stamina. So, during the year when events happen; the local sports teams play; the Arts are on stage and screen; and just a nice day beckons, Cleveland comes through with many choices and venues. That is what this book is about. The Cleveland that is perhaps unexpected. The amount of choices: Where to go, What to do, Where to Stay, What to see, so much so that repeated excursions are needed, And if only one trip to Cleveland is possible then the happy duty is making some choices.

Cleveland, Location

As much as any American City, Cleveland is defined by its location along Lake Erie. The massive Glaziers of the last Ice Age left behind depressions of the earth's crust into which the melting fresh water collected and produced the five inland fresh water seas that we call Great Lakes. Erie is the smallest of the five, and the shallowest. Its mass is aligned along the west to east axis of the prevailing continental winds, such that it caries moisture, both moderating and extreme.

The extreme, of course is the famous Lake Effect Snows that come when the arctic cold air chugs across the warm water of Great Lake Erie, and then meets the land mass and unloads is moisture. It is one of the world's most unique weather phenomena. Anyone from Buffalo, NY would scoff at the effect it has on Cleveland, and that is a given. However it does illustrate the power of Great Lake Erie and how it affects the climate of Cleveland and Northeast Ohio.

By example, the shores of Lake Erie have been for centuries known for the productions of grapes. Mostly these grapes have been the hearty native grapes discounted by snobs as being less than outstanding. The truth is told most of the grape stocks of Europe are now the North American varieties grafted with the disease susceptible Old World varieties. Grapes grow well in Northeast Ohio, along with other temperature sensitive crops because Great Lake Erie moderates the harsh continental climate.

This explains how Cleveland and Cuyahoga County sit in the midst of a great agricultural region in Northeast Ohio. And, in the here and now, the bounties of those farms are reappearing on a regular basis in the menus of some of the country's best and brightest Chefs. Beautiful fresh produce from a new crop of dynamic farmers who are rediscovering ancient ways of farming from neighbors like the largest population of Amish in America in nearby Holmes County; updating modern practices to be more efficient and more kind to the environment, and raising heritage crops and critters that are appearing in Cleveland's creative restaurants in ways not ever seen or tasted before.

A lot of this ebook is about eating in Cleveland, and well it should be. Going to Cleveland should never, as of now, include trips to national chain restaurants. That would be an utter waste of a good trip to Cleveland. However, that does not mean putting most of the budget into Chef-centric locations with the accompanying price. We have included places to eat that are Cleveland inside and out, offering unique flavors, for what can only be called cheap. That is where we land in this book. Cleveland offers travelers a myriad of choices, some are even luxurious, but expensive is not a part of the Cleveland story -- unless one wants it to be. Simply put, much of the best of Cleveland is cheap or free.

Cleveland Climate

We all suppose it is easy to lump the climate of Cleveland into the amorphous mass of Continental North American four seasons climate. With each season known more for its hazards and bad spells than for anything delightful and rewarding. That would be something less than insightful. Cleveland can beguile with warm days, cool nights, colorful Falls, and that special kind of snowy filigree that fills a back yard after a Christmas Eve snow as depicted in the classic holiday movie *A Christmas Story*, filmed in Tremont

July is typically the warmest month with an average temperature of 71.9 °F (22.2 °C), however, temperatures in the high 80s to low 90s °F with relatively high humidity are not unusual.
January is typically the coldest month with an average temperature of 25.7 °F (−3.5 °C). Winters are cold, with

a handful of heavy snowfalls, and the occasional windchill factor below 0 °F.

The east side of Cleveland also experiences "Lake Effect" snow from mid-November until the surface of Lake Erie freezes, typically by early February. This creates snowfall due to the city's location on Lake Erie's southern shore, where the shoreline shifts from an east-west direction to a northeast-southwest orientation.

Cleveland's autumn season is probably its most moderate weather, with high-60-degree temperatures and low humidity through the end of October.

Cleveland History

Cleveland is a culturally diverse city. The region was home to Original peoples of the ancient past who lived by combining hunting, gathering, and eventually farming in sustainable ways that lasted through the centuries. According to the first European explorers the preferable low lands along Lake Erie were all but devoid of human habitation when they arrived in the 17th century. Because so much of the precious heritage of these peoples was lost to the oblivious agricultural practices beginning in the early 19th century it is difficult for modern archaeologists to uncover all the sites and artifacts of the past. We do know that in the centuries before the arrival of Europeans the area was well populated with villages and 'towns' complete with ceremonial structures, such as Mounds, and a thriving culture.

Some speculation places the aggressive warlike behavior of the so-called Iroquois Nation that overran the local populations and led to collapse. Though this theory has some merit it does not take into account the devastating effects of the diseases Europeans introduced into North America beginning in the century just before. It may be true, that a combination of the two events led to the great decrease in Native populations, but no definitive narrative has been established.

The coming of Europeans put Ohio and Northeast Ohio into the realm of their conquests and conflicts. The Great Lakes were caught up in these conflicts because they offered the widest and best transportation for the lucrative Fur Trade and then a century later the burgeoning Midwest farms that produced their own chance for wealth. The European Colonial conflicts eventually culminated in the first true World War, the Seven Years War which in America is pejoratively recalled as the French and Indian War.

Then the American Revolution impacted the area when afterwards the region was deeded over to Connecticut Yankee pro-Revolution farmers who had been burned out of their farms by the British. Hence the name, the Firelands which is used commonly to this day to describe the Western Reserve of Northeast Ohio. The next conflict of European origin was the War of 1812, where the Great Lakes again were a natural focal point of the conflict between Great Britain with British America against the United States of America.

Zars

Eventually these conflicts ended, and the region was quickly swept up in the Westward push of land hungry Americans eager to farm and other enterprises. It is in the context of expansion and relocation that Cleveland was first envisioned as a venture during the Federal era. The whole practice of buying and selling land as a means to wealth was all but invented in North America by Americans primarily of British heritage who turned their back on the Old World practice of amassing land ownership as the primary means to status and wealth.

Beginning in Colonial times owners of vast, distant land found they could sell their exploitative ownership to a burgeoning population. Cleveland was envisioned as the principal city of a great agricultural and trading center belonging to the Western reaches of Connecticut. The ownership of the land of Cleveland by the Connecticut Land Company was obtained by political power and expediency. This Connecticut Company included General Moses Cleaveland, a Revolutionary War veteran, surveyor and namesake of Ohio's largest city.

Moses Cleaveland

Not long after the Connecticut Company was formed simple common sense and the new national government abandoned the idea of the original 13 states elongating into continental units. As for the 'a' in General Cleaveland's name, it was said typesetters who needed more space dropped it from the city's name in the 19th century. We tend to think it was just aesthetics. Dropping the 'a' didn't change the pronunciation, and is obviously more symmetric.

One of the greatest governing documents of the American epoch is the often overlooked Northwest Ordinance. Though it seems not much more than a recipe for attaining statehood for Americans as they took a big swath of North America, it can be missed how the Ordinance establishes the absolute primacy of constitutional democratic representative republican government: Self-governance as a fundamental right wherever American citizens have the requisite populations. This is first time that an expanding power imbued all of its citizens with the same rights as the original governances. Doing so without any deference to heritage or history.

Ohio was one of the first states to take advantage of the Northwest Ordinance and entered the Union as an equal state in 1803. Cleveland was established in the years leading to statehood and was, as indicated, an entrepreneurial opportunity. Up to this point almost all American cities were located where natural features dictated, such as rivers meeting ocean with good harbors. The exception was Washington, District of Columbia being platted by government degree. Beginning with places like Cleveland, the entire idea of civilization could exist because it offered the best place for making money by selling land and houses got under way.

Because Cleveland originates in enterprise it seems inevitable that for the whole of the 19th century an inexorable increase in wealth culminated in the late 19th century and early 20th centuries when Cleveland became home to the most millionaires on earth. At the same time it was home to wave after wave of aspiring newcomers, both national and international. That fact more than any other is the central reality present in today's Cleveland.

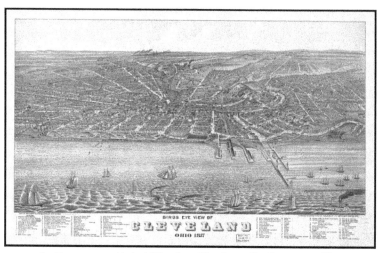

A. Ruger, artist. Lith. by Shober & Carqueville

The mix of Colonial American pioneers; Western and Eastern European immigrants; African American and Latin American migrants, and a wide array of immigrants from all over the world are the contours of Cleveland's culture. The belief in rectifying classic European culture by the landed and industrial American Protestants of the 19th century is still evident in the acclaimed cultural institutions such as the Cleveland Symphony Orchestra.

The Old World heritage of immigrants manifests throughout Cleveland culture in festivals, live music and ethnic food all found at churches, temples, synagogues, mosques, and just on the street. Migrant populations from the South, both African American and Latin America also imbue Cleveland culture with food, music, art and language. The end result is a kaleidoscope culture that seems commonplace at times to the citizens of Cleveland, however it is anything but.

This poly-cultural environment, if you will, may be why Cleveland is generally considered one of the most dynamic and interesting places to visit. Add in an abundance of outside recreational places and activities and it is easy to see how tourism and travel are essential to the region's economy.

At the same time there is no hiding that Cleveland has suffered through repeated challenges in the 20th and early 21st century. The predicament of race and prejudice is no less evident in Cleveland than anywhere else in America. Cleveland has moved more and more toward reconciliation and co-operation beyond race – more than other large American cities, but with one economic dislocation after another the challenges remain. In so much as the central city neighborhoods are in revitalization it is possible that not all citizens of Cleveland will participate. More dislocation for citizens whose only disqualification for shared economic revitalization is their race or heritage would not just be a shame—it would be a sin.

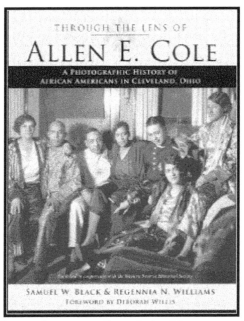

Through-Lens-Allen-Cole-Photograph

During the recent period of revitalization four political figures stand out. All were Mayors of Cleveland. Beginning with Mayor Carl Stokes, the first African American mayor of a major American city. Dennis Kucinich, the youngest mayor at that time of a major American city, followed him. Kucinich, suffered through a difficult mayoralty that included a recall effort. Eventually he became a US Congressman, ran for President, and remains a voice for progressive politics. George Voinovich followed Kucinich.

Voinovich went onto be elected Governor of Ohio and then US Senator. His success was due in no small part because under his watch Cleveland kept growing and was financially stable.

The one that may be the most interesting though is Mayor Michael R. White, the second youngest person to become Mayor of Cleveland and the second African American. He served the longest duration of any Cleveland Mayor (or so it seems). He could have won a forth term, but declined to do so.

He moved to Ohio's Amish Country to raise Alpacas and wine grapes. His seeming willingness to truncate his political career was linked to the criminal conviction of some close associates. So much so, that for years the standard line was Michael White was awaiting the inevitable results of an ongoing Federal investigation into city corruption.

Well, that other shoe to drop has dangled for nearly a decade, and it can pretty much assumed there will be no charges.

What is so fascinating is that Mayor White, who was generally considered in line for National political attention, would step away to run a farm and now a winery as well. When visiting Cleveland it is obvious that much of the new Cleveland is centered in the Gateway District with its Stadiums, restaurants, and entertainment. All happened under Michael White's leadership, and are essential to Cleveland's ability to survive and thrive.

Cleveland Attractions

When in Cleveland the basics list of 'must-see, must-do' places and activities, in no particular order include: The Big Five" orchestra, the World Famous **Cleveland Symphonhy Orchestra** and its sublime home at Severance Hall. Part of the attending a performance is being in the **University Circle** district. University Circle is Cleveland's other civic center, home to world class arts, museums, university, and health centers.

University Circle is also home to the world-renowned art museum **The Cleveland Museum of Art**. Since the early Twentieth Century the Neo-Classical edifice of the Museum and its gorgeous setting on Wade Park's Lake in University Circle are inviting in their own right. Inside is a massive collection of Art spanning centuries, continents, mediums and styles. Of special note is their collection of Asian and Egyptian Art demonstrating an ongoing interest in Art beyond Europe

Cleveland's downtown is home to the second largest performing arts center in the United States, **Playhouse Square Center**. Yes, that is second only to Broadway. Obviously, Chicago holds its own, no doubt, but this fabulous resource has been supported by Clevelanders for decades and that tradition continues in the year ahead with a remarkable schedule of Broadway Original Productions, Broadway Touring Productions, and Professional Productions that originate in Cleveland.

The Rock and Roll Hall of Fame and Museum in downtown on the shores of Lake Erie is only 20 years old in 2013, but it has already established itself as a World Renowned destination in America. The fact it is located in Cleveland and the subsequent controversy of the design and construction of the Museum buildings -- even the selection of inductees has waned over time. Now, it functions as a repository and research center for a big slice of American Culture. It also remains focused on Artists who are nearing or are well into their golden years. (Those who are still alive)

At some point the Hall will have to become something of a memorial and less of a living hall of fame, by nature. The issue is can it stay meaningful to new generations who may think of the Rock and Roll Hall of Fame belonging to a time and to people who have come and gone? That is not their mission, as we understand it, and lately the Hall has made some inroads in capturing and preserving popular music from the 21st Century. Regardless of its ability to stay just behind the wake of what is hip and now, the Hall is always as fascinating as the artists and their music.

The Great Lakes Science Center/Omnimax Theater is immediately adjacent lakeside to the Rock and Roll Hall of Fame and First Energy Stadium home of the NFL Cleveland Browns. The Great Lake Science Center is one of Nation's best. It was built about ten years after the Hall, and the attraction of the full sized Ominmax Theater is still a top draw. The Center has benefited from its relationship with the nearby Cleveland NASA facility and Ohio's legendary astronaut and Senator the late John Glenn with the NASA Glen Visitor Center. The Great Lakes Science Center also includes the Laker Steamship William G Mather.

The Cleveland Museum of Natural History
1 Wade Oval Drive Cleveland, Ohio 44106

University Circle is home to many of Cleveland's best public attractions. The Cleveland Museum of Natural History which amidst the lawns and gardens of the Circle is popular year round. The museum offers year round attractions in the permanent collection and special displays and shows. Not the least of which is the great dog hero, Balto the Husky.

Balto was the lead sled dog for the last treacherous leg of the delivery of diphtheria serum to Nome, Alaska. The re-creation of that dog sled delivery of life saving medicine became the annual Iditirod Sled Dog race in Alaska. Though Balto was not the only heroic dog to save Nome – just as important if not more so is the extraordinary story of lead dog Togo (and all of the dogs of that heroic run) -- what set Balto apart for Cleveland is the fact that Balto is a rescued dog and not just a dog rescuer.

When Blato's nationwide fame was fading he and other dog companions ended up in a Los Angeles freak show. Then Clevelander George Kimble, a successful businessman and one time famous prizefighter discovered Blato's desperate situation. He raised the funds needed to purchase Balto along with the other dogs from the show operator with the help of thousands of Cleveland children in a short period of time. An accomplishment that would be dazzling even with today's online social fundraising. Eventually Balto and his mates were kept in good condition and well cared for at the Cleveland Zoological Gardens, but not before a legendary parade in Cleveland to honor all of the dogs. Balto passed away at the age of 14, and his remains were taxidermy for display.

Balto

In 2017 Balto went back to Alaska for the first time in a half of a century for a display recounting the purchase of Alaska from Russia, the so-called Seward's Folly. The interesting relationship of the Untied States and Russia is as timely today, as ever. Balto is joined by Togo for this display in the Polar Bear Garden at the Anchorage Museum. When it is over, Balto will return to his home in Cleveland.

The Cleveland Botanical Garden
11030 East Boulevard Cleveland Ohio 44106

One of the gems of Cleveland public spaces, the Cleveland Botanical Garden located in University Circle offers year round displays of exquisite plants and plantings on the 10 acres of gardens and the 18,000 square foot Elanor Smith Armstrong glass house. To go along with the displays the CBG hosts numerous events and occasions throughout the year. Besides providing a delightful place to enjoy, the CBG is deeply involved with the Cleveland community. Its wide support has made it possible to do such important programs as the annual Green Corp. an urban farming program for inner city Teens, and an applied research program to turn abandoned city property into green infrastructure.

A Christmas Story House and Visitors Center
3159 W 11th St, Cleveland, OH 44109

Back in 1988 when *A Christmas Story* was released, it was reviewed as a better-than-average version of the family Christmas time movie, with a saucy naughtiness that author the late Jean Shepard used to spice up his original childhood memoir short story. Deftly Canadian filmmaker the late Bob Clark remained true to Shepard's voice, even to the point that Shepard was the voice-over that knits the whole story together. As much as any movie, *A Christmas Story* demonstrates what can be accomplished when the Writer and Director are on the same page. And the results have been, and this is an understatement, monumental.

Not only did the engaging story of potty mouthed grade schoolers in a winter time setting inspire two Colorado kids to animate their take on the movie's milieu, and call it South Park after their childhood everwinter suburban habitat, but the repeated Christmas Eve and Day playing of *A Christmas Story* on the Turner Network is now a Christmas tradition that is being handed down from generation to generation. In it's own way A Christmas Story is as much a business center unto itself as the Harry Potter sagas are. Though *A Christmas Story* is a one-off, the sequels not withstanding.

The setting of the Movie is Shepard's gauzy memory of his boyhood Hammond, Indiana/Chicagoland. However, the movie was shot both in Cleveland and Toronto. The Cleveland location of the utmost importance is the house in Tremont, sitting on the escarpment above the Cuyahoga river valley. This is the house that has become, in its own right, a cultural icon complete with the Major Award illuminated Stripper's Leg lamp perfectly placed in the front window. A few steps away from the front porch on West 11th Street is the Visitor Center.

Cleveland Metroparks Zoo

One of the best city zoos in America, the Cleveland Metro Park Zoo has updated its habitats into humane environments for their animal inhabitants. And they have put an even greater focus on education and public awareness so that the Mission of Environmental preservation is at the forefront. Always a wonderful time for any age, the Cleveland Metropark Zoo is especially joyous with children along for a day.

A rather large Zoo that takes up over 70 acres, the Cleveland Metropark Zoo offers free tram rides. Nonetheless, expect to spend a full day seeing the diverse and fascinating natural exhibits that range from tropical rain forest, to the Northern world of the Wolf. This much to see may mean some amount of walking. Be prepared with comfortable shoes and hydration liquids. The whole zoo is ADA accessible.

Crawford Auto-Aviation Museum
10825 East Blvd, Cleveland, OH 44106

As of now, The Crawford Auto-Aviation Museum is part of the cultural richness of University Circle. There has been some speculation that it may move closer to downtown at the Burke Lakefront Airport. Wherever the Crawford is, it represents a truly eclectic collection of rare automobiles many with a direct connection to the legendary history of Cleveland's automotive history. Like other parts of the Midwest, Cleveland shared in the rich early history of American automotive manufacture, before consolidation centered most of the carmakers in Detroit. Like Detroit, Cleveland had access to natural resources, rail transportation and a ready work force. The end result is a fascinating history of pre-1940s automobiles mostly, mixed with cars all the way into the 21st Century.

Cleveland Events 2020

Brite Winter 2/2020
An annual music, art, food and beer festival along the West bank of the Flats. Outdoors. In Winter. In Cleveland. Last year: 393 Bands, 100K+ festival goers.

Kurentovanje 2/2020
The Slovenian way of scarring away winter and bringing in Spring with food, dance, something to drink, music, more food and scary monsters to get the job done.

St. Patrick's Day. 3/2020.
One of the largest in America, this is Saint Pat's done Cleveland style. Which, just means a very big, very exciting, party.

Cleveland International Film Festival. 3-4/2020
With the focus on Socially relevant films, and works
from Israel, Central and Eastern Europe. All in one
location at the Terminal Tower downtown.

The Cleveland Thyagaraja Festival. 4/2020
All is not just Rock n Roll and Polkas in Cleveland. This
festival of Classic India music and dance is the largest
in the world outside of India. At Cleveland State
University.

Dingus Day. The Monday after Easter 2020
A Polish happening, this is one of the best Dingus
Days in the US. Rapidly becoming an almost as
popular bookend to Mardi Gras, Numerous locations
throughout Cleveland.

Memorial Day 2020
One of the highlights is the renowned Berea National
Rib Cook-Off at the Cuyahoga County Fairgrounds.

Cleveland Asian Festival 5/2020
The ethnic neighborhood of Asia Town just east of
Downtown is home to this celebration of Asian
Americans, their cultures, and contributions to
Cleveland and America. Great food, of course.

Larchemere Porch Festival 6/2020
Americans love their porches, and so Larchemere the hipper East side Cleveland neighborhood turns porches into band stands, and front lawns, sidewalks and city streets into a festival venue.

Pride in the Cle. 6/2020
Cleveland's LGBTQ+ community celebrates in that exuberant Cleveland way that is for everyone. As such the popular parade is surrounded by extra events, of entertainment, education, and activism. And the fun spills over into numerous Cleveland night spots.

Burning River Festival 6/2020
Maestro Newman wrote of the long ago Cuyahoga in Cleveland:
"The Lord can make you tumble, the Lord can make you turn.
The Lord can make you overflow,
but the Lord can't make you Burn."
So, clean it up, celebrate all Environmental causes and throw a party along the banks of Cleveland's river.
In The Flats.

Parade The Circle – Summer Solstice 6/2020
The Cleveland Museum of the Arts celebrates Art and Creativity with a parade on the Wade Oval. All are invited, except for motor vehicles, or branding signage. Fun for kids, lots of food, and yes, beer. University Circle.

Cleveland Jazz Festival 6/2020
One of the longest running and best in the country, the Cleveland Jazz Festival reaffirms Cleveland's status as a Jazz city.
Playhouse Square.

Waterloo Arts Festival 6/2020
The Waterloo Art District holds an annual event to celebrate their mile long corridor of Art, Artists, and the creative side of things.

Taste of Tremont 07/2020
Later on you may notice a lot of great Tremont places to eat and have in this city guide. This event is sort of the Cliff Note's of imbibing Tremont.
Fun for the whole family. Especially if the family likes good food.

Labor Day Weekend 2017
Cleveland National Air Show Labor
Burke Lakefront Airport

Oktoberfest 9/2020
Cuyahoga County Fairgrounds,
City of Berea

Village Peddler Festival 9/2020
A delightful Farm Park is the backdrop for over 150
'peddlers' with items of all kinds, and all expertly
made. Definitely family fun
Lake Metroparks Farmpark, City of Kirtland

Sparx City Hop 9/2020
A free one day self-directed tour of Cleveland's art
and creative community. Spread out over locations
from Ohio City to University Circle, all made possible
by the free rides on the Blue, Red and Green Line city
trolleys.
Various locations, and Downtown Cleveland

Halloween Season 10/2020
Boo at the Zoo
Cleveland Metroparks Zoo
The Rain Forest, Cleveland's Old Brooklyn
neighborhood

Playhouse Square Theater Tour 10/2020
1519 Euclid Ave Cleveland, OH 44115
Admission: Free
With five fully restored historic theaters (built 1921-22), Playhouse Square is the largest theater restoration project in the world.

Cleveland Beer Week
Various Cleveland neighborhoods

I-X Christmas Connection 11/2020
I-X Center, Cleveland's West
Park neighborhood

Winterfest 11/2020
The Saturday after Thanksgiving kick off to the Downtown Cleveland Holiday season, Winterfest is all kinds of fun. And do not get confused. The major downtown department stores are gone, but there is plenty of shopping and bargains at Tower City and across downtown.
Various locations, Downtown Cleveland

Glow Winter Spectacular 11-12/2020
Cleveland Botanical Garden,
Cleveland's University Circle neighborhood

Holiday Circle Fest
Various locations, Cleveland's
University Circle neighborhood

The Polar Express 11-12/2020
Cuyahoga Valley Scenic Railroad.
Inspired by the ever more beloved Holiday Classic
book and movie, the Cuyahoga Valley Railroad is
perfect to emulate the ride to the North Pole and
Santa through Cleveland's National Park. The
excursion includes readings from the book, music
from the movie, and of course hot chocolate and
cookies.

As you can imagine, tickets are scooped up fast, so
please check for availability online.

Getting to Cleveland

Like many Midwestern cities, Cleveland's transportation is car based, but not exclusively so. When it comes to cars, the banks of Lake Erie and the fact Cleveland sits on it bank, makes the overall geometry that of a half-circle. (Like Chicago) So, the general directions of freeways are east and west, north and south on a half-wheel with Cleveland at the hub. As in all American freeway numerations, the odd numbers are generally north and south and the even numbers are east and west. The Ohio Turnpike I-80 skirts the city to the south on its way to Pennsylvania. In enters the western edge of Greater Cleveland as Interstate 80-90. These two great east-west freeways share the same lanes until they permanently divide just to the west of Cleveland, with I-90 continuing on to downtown Cleveland; the northeastern suburbs, and onto New England. Interstate 80 remains the Ohio Turnpike until it diverges near Youngstown just before Pennsylvania on its way to New York City. At that point I-80 becomes a non-toll freeway through the northern tier of Pennsylvania, Northern New Jersey and then to New York City. The Ohio Turnpike continues to the Pennsylvania Turnpike as Interstate 76.

The north south freeways all have 7 as a first number. Interstate 71 goes to Columbus and then to Cincinnati and Interstate 75 (the nation's second longest freeway that connects Michigan to Florida). Interstate 77 stays to the east side of Ohio and on to the Appalachian south of West Virginia, Virginia, North Carolina and South Carolina.

Among these four major routes are some connector freeways: The Interbelt freeway that traverses from the east side of downtown south to the Interstate 80. Interstate 480 offers a belt way like bypass from the west side to the east side of Greater Cleveland where it connected to Interstate 80, the Ohio Turnpike. US 20 leaves downtown west bound along Lake Erie as a freeway before becoming a surface arterial on its way to Lakeland, Ohio.

Train:

Amtrak Station is located near the Lake near the NFL Brown's Stadium and the Rock and Roll Hall of Fame. Unfortunately, most Amtrak routes serving Cleveland arrive and depart between the early morning hours of 1:00 - 4:00 a.m. On cold nights, it may be the most miserable place to catch a train in America. In so many ways, Amtrak to Cleveland is not a great choice.

This is astounding when one considers that the whole reason for Terminal Tower and Tower City was to be the Grand Central and Penn Station combined of Cleveland. Today's station is a mere approximation of a railway station with its suburbanesque minimal architecture. It's just depressing.

Anyhow, Amtrak's Capitol Limited from Washington, D.C. or Chicago and Lake Shore Limited from New York, Boston or Chicago stop in Cleveland.

The Cuyahoga Valley Scenic Railway is a non-profit organization that operates an excursion train through the Cuyahoga Valley National Park in cooperation with the National Park Service. The train has a northern most stop south of Cleveland in Independence Ohio. It continues through the Cuyahoga Valley National Park to its southern terminus in North Akron, Ohio.

The train operates on a Wednesday through Sunday schedule during the warm weather months. With the planned completion of the Ohio & Erie Canal Towpath Trail, folks on bikes and hikers will be able to go from downtown Flats and through the Cuyahoga Valley National Park on their way to New Philadelphia and Ohio's Amish Country. That is why the CVSR offers a popular Bike Aboard program to take advantage of the scenic railway as part of a National Park excursion in scenic Northeastern Ohio.

Bus:

The Greyhound station in Cleveland is just the opposite of the Amtrak Station. It is located in downtown, and is one of the best examples of late Deco Streamline Moderne style of architecture in the City.

Designed by architect William Strudwick Arrasmith, it was the last of his work for Greyhound, and perhaps the best. It retains much of its original look even after restoration by Greyhound. Even if your not going Greyhound, peek inside to get the full feel of its intended sensations of speed and Deco influenced mechanization. Greyhound offers bus service from many U.S. cities.

Airplane:

Cleveland Hopkins International Airport (CLE) Ohio's largest and Cleveland's main airport is located on the southwest west side of the city. It is the oldest Municipal Airport in the country opening in 1925. The airport is served by major domestic airlines including United and Southwest. The RTA Red Line Rapid Transit provides frequent and fast rail service from inside the airport to the heart of downtown in roughly 22 minutes.

Akron-Canton Regional Airport. Visitors could also use this airport, which is served by regional airline affiliates and is a 45-minute drive from Cleveland.

Boat:

In recent years the interest in Cruising on the Great Lakes has burgeoned. The number of Great Lakes Cruise Ships is the highest it has been since the heyday of cruise ships on the Great Lakes in the early 20th century. Great Lakes Cruises have easy to reach embarkations; numerous major cities for ports of call; historic sites to visit, natural wonders along the Lakes, and of course the Great Lakes themselves that afford a sea going vista far from the shore, while still in protected waters.

Most cruises that come to Lake Erie naturally include Cleveland on their Itinerary.

Getting Around Cleveland

Car:

Cleveland might be one of the easiest cities in the world to navigate. There are almost no one-way streets. Traffic is generally not a problem relative to other major U.S. metro areas. Throughout the downtown area, purple signs direct visitors to let you know where you are and what district you are in.

The streets that run north-south are numbered, except for Ontario Street (the north-south street bisecting Public Square). Numbered Streets are named as "West", west of Ontario and "East", east of Ontario. (Broadview Road becomes the primary geographic boundary between 'East' and 'West' addresses to the south of the city.)

The major east-west streets are generally named as "Avenues". The arterials and surface streets are among the easier drives in any American City. Because Cleveland is located on a wide coastal plain, it has few elevations. And with only the Cuyahoga River, and Rocky River to the west offering any kind of bridgeable barrier, most of the streets are smartly laid out.

Downtown boasts wide boulevards in keeping with its 19th century heritage. Organic old town streets are just not a part of Cleveland, because it is a planned city. In and around downtown the main movement is east and west. Along this axis are the important east side arterials: St. Claire, Superior, and Euclid. All originate in downtown. To the west are Detroit, the once main road to the city of Detroit and Lorain. North and south are more dependent on the Interstates. West 25th directs southbound through most of the city. The east has numbered streets that head north and south include arterials. Beyond Cleveland the suburbs are interconnected by the same freeway/arterial system.

Finding an address is simple as well. Numbers on north-south streets increase as you head south from Lake Erie, numbers on east-west streets increase as you head away from downtown and coincide with the numbered streets (i.e. 6500 Detroit Ave is located at the corner of Detroit Ave and W 65th St). Odd number addresses on north-south streets are for buildings on the east side of the street, and even number addresses are on the west side; on the west side of Cleveland, odd addresses on east-west streets are located on the south side of the street, while even addresses are on the north side--the reverse is true for east-west streets on the east side of Cleveland. This addressing scheme continues into most of the suburbs (some exceptions include Berea and Bedford) and even most cities and townships in Lake and Lorain Counties.

Most of the city is laid out in grids and has very clear signage enabling you to easily know where you are. Throughout the area, signs are thoroughly placed to indicate the route to the nearest major freeway, making the city visitor-friendly.

Public Transportation

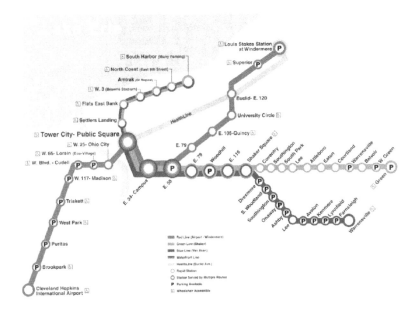

Cleveland has a surprisingly good public transportation system. It is reasonably priced and offers travelers inexpensive and flexible one day passes that are readily available at the card pass kiosks. As of publication the price is $5.00. This pass includes all forms of public transpiration including the light and heavy rail lines, the new BRT line from downtown to University Circle called the Health Line, and all buses

The Cleveland area is served by a public bus and rail transit system called the Regional Transit Authority or RTA. The rail portion consists of two light rail lines, the Green and Blue Lines that extend to eastern and southern suburbs; and a heavy rail line, the Red Line that services the eastern side out to University Circle and west to Cleveland Hopkins International Airport Because Cleveland is a kind of hub and spoke city layout, buses and trains head for downtown from all directions. The major destinations of this ebook; Ohio City, Tremont, University Circle, Little Italy, and downtown Cleveland all offer ample public transpiration options. For the making of this book, as all of our books, no car was employed.

We relied on the Red Line to Ohio City and buses over to Tremont. (It's a nice walk, as well) To the west buses work Lorain and Detroit regularly every day of the week.

Downtown Motor Trolleys offer day and evening free service to almost all of downtown. They are color coded, and easy to pick up at numerous stops along their routes.

The trolleys use a Letter designation that sort of relates to the purpose of the route. The C trolley loops from the JACK Casino. Its hours are centered in the evenings. The B line goes through Cleveland's business district, and its hours are daylight and early evening based on workdays. The E line heads to Cleveland State University mostly by using Euclid. Its hours are daylight and early evenings. There are two more routes. Both go to the Lakeside and its attractions, such as the Rock and Roll Hall of Fame and the Browns football stadium.

The Trolleys are a bit ersatz, with brass fittings and solid wood seats, but the locals don't see them as a tourist attraction and regularly use the free trolley system to get around downtown.

The Waterfront Line, a short track light rail line specifically caters to tourists and sports fans as it travels from Tower City Center to the Flats Entertainment District, Cleveland Browns Stadium, Great Lakes Science Center, the Rock and Roll Hall of Fame, and Burke Lakefront Airport. To the east and southeast we had many choices including the two light rail lines, and the new Health Line Rapid Bus Transportation. The Health Line is Bus Rapid Transit and is considered a model for the rest of the country. It has made the commute from downtown east to the numerous health industry related activities near University Circle a much quicker ride. The buses are new articulating double coaches that resemble in size and speed modern streetcars.

The success of this BRT is not just in faster, easier transportation, but in economics, as well. Already along the Health Line new businesses are springing up indicative of increased economic activity in a corridor that was once thought to be a lost cause between downtown and University Circle.

The Health Line has its own center lanes with dedicated ground level platforms and an 'on your honor' payment system that does not require each passenger 's ticket submission. The ride is quick and easy.

Bicycle:

Greater Cleveland is expanding its bicycle trails and bicycle paths throughout the city. In addition, the city has numerous bicycle shops, mostly located on the near west side, and a bicycle co-op. For more information on biking in Cleveland, visit Bike Cleveland.

The popularity of using bicycles is growing, and a raft of new businesses catering to bicycling commuters, touring, and exercise are available.

For an adventure excursion that originates in Cleveland and take riders to the heart of Ohio's Amish Country there is the Ohio & Erie Canal Towpath trail for bikes and hikers. This trail, part of an extensive system of rails to trails and towpath trails in Ohio. It starts in downtown Cleveland, going south through the Cuyahoga Valley National Park and Akron to New Philadelphia and Ohio's Amish Country.

Cleveland Architecture:

We are sorry if this sounds like a key stuck on repeat, but Cleveland's attributes are seriously overlooked. Architecture is one of those things.

Because it was a boom town for so much of the 19th and early 20th century Cleveland ended up with numerous examples of monumental civic and enterprise architecture. There was a slowdown toward the end of the last century when major structures were less frequent. Eventually Cleveland optimism returned with a spate of public structures, many related to the local Sports teams along with a renewed appreciation of the whole history of architecture in Cleveland.

The range of architecture starts in the Federal Era at the planned beginnings of Cleveland, and spans to the post-structalist work of Frank Gehry. In-between are numerous examples of nineteenth and early twentieth century works reflecting the American interest in European epoch such a neo-classic Greek revival, Italianate, and Beaux Arts. Victoriana including the handsome Eastlake Style is well represented in Cleveland. Twentieth century styles such as Craftsman, and Art Deco are numerous. Modern and Post Modern buildings are widely present as well.

Frank Gehry designed this building, using his trademark undulating forms, including brick.

Of special interest is the remarkable survival of vernacular houses and styles in the neighborhoods. Many Victorian era houses built for working class residents remain in remarkable condition. Often times these lower valued houses were the first to be eliminated when neighborhoods underwent unwanted changes. The grander houses, in many cities, survived more readily because of their locations and perceived value.

Walking around neighborhoods such as Ohio City or Tremont is a centuries worth of education in everyday architecture ranging from the simple brick houses for railroad employees to late twentieth century Modernist residences that take advantage of views across the Cuyahoga to downtown Cleveland. In between are a myriad of styles, most of which appealed to working class families who had attained a chance for a better level of housing thanks to the growth in the local economy.

Terminal Tower

At the time it was built in 1929, Terminal Tower was the second tallest building in the world and now the second tallest in Cleveland. Terminal Tower is the skyscraper of Tower City Center, located on Public Square. Originally built as the Cleveland Union Terminal Railroad Station, Tower City Center houses retail shops and offices. The lower level serves as the main hub of the RTA Rapid Lines, Cleveland's light-rail transit system.

Arcades

Although arcades exist in several North American cities, few—if any—compare to the grandeur of The Arcade in Cleveland. Built in 1890, construction was financed by John D. Rockefeller, Marcus Hanna, and

several other wealthy Clevelanders of the day. The structure includes a five-story; sky lighted atrium with extensive metal decorative work as well as two nine-story towers, one each on Euclid and Superior Avenues. In the past decade, the structure was renovated as a Hyatt Regency Hotel. The cost of the project was approximately $875,000 and would be impossible to replicate today. Fittingly The Arcade was the first building in Cleveland to be placed on the National Register of Historic Places.

The Rock and Roll Hall of Fame and Museum

I.M. Pei's under appreciated masterpiece. Yes, we know Pei himself was not overly excited by his RnRHOF. However, few museums ever built are as iconic and functional as this structure. His Lourve

Pyramid looks exactly what it is: A modern glass pyramid dropped like some kind of high priced Christmas ornament in front of a massive Beau Arts caprice. The Rock and Roll Hall of Fame seems to be the whole loaf that the Pyramid slice was cut from.

Formerly known as the Lorain-Carnegie Bridge, the Hope Memorial Bridge was named for famous actor/comedian and native Clevelander Bob Hope's father, who worked on its construction. This well-known and much-photographed bridge is framed by four art deco pylon sculptures portraying the evolution of forms of ground transportation. Along with a large number of jack-knife and lift bridges along the Cuyahoga River, one of the world's few remaining "Swing Bridges" is still in use, connecting the east and west banks of The Flats entertainment district.

University Circle Attractions

Cleveland Art

As it was described to us, a lot of the revitalization of the Cleveland neighborhoods is in part to the ability of local artists and creators to find low cost spaces, move in, and kick start a neighborhood. This is not the whole story, of course, because so much else of it is the Millennial Generation seeking to live in affordable and full service urban settings, when at the same time many retiring Baby Boomers choosing the inner core of the City as the place to retire instead of an isolated geriatric community. Whatever the reasons, the Art Community in Cleveland has had an impact by being well supported by the Clevelanders who appreciate Art and the work of creative people. That is no small reason to visit Cleveland. As for the galleries and destinations, here are the big ones:

Cleveland Museum of Art,

 A world-renowned collection of Asian art, plus Greek and Roman statuary and modern art are exhibited at this free art museum. The crown jewels of the museum are its stunning collections of medieval armor and an original casting of Auguste Rodin's The Thinker.

MOCA - Museum of Contemporary Art

MOCA is free to all visitors on Friday. Designed by internationally acclaimed architect and Harvard Professor Farshid Moussavi, this newest of Cleveland's art museums also is intended as a catalyst for creativity and growth in Cleveland. So far it has provided meaningful space to many contemporary artists who deserve a curated exhibition. However, MOCA does pose the opposite end of the spectrum of Art for Urban Renewal. In the sense the organic Art-to-Enterprise phenomena that have sprung up across the Cleveland are by definition unplanned and focused on neighborhoods lacking in many ways, contemporary museums like MOCA must be located in established arts destinations, such as the University Circle area.

Cleveland Public Art - This non-profit organization sponsors art projects throughout the city, including the spires and vegetable wall near Progressive Field, the murals on Tremont School, and the Wade Oval gate at the Cleveland Botanical Garden. The organization is headquartered in Ohio City.

Rockefeller Cultural Gardens

The Gardens represent Cleveland's diverse and rich ethno-cultural mosaic along a picturesque winding road, connecting University Circle to I-90 via MLK Blvd.
The Children's Museum, 10730 Euclid Ave, +1
216 791-KIDS
Cleveland Museum of Natural History
Located in University Circle, the museum has exhibits ranging from dinosaurs to a working observatory.
 The Crawford Auto-Aviation Museum
Connected to the Western Reserve Historical Society Museum in University Circle, this is a must-visit museum for the classic car fan.
The Cleveland Botanical Gardens Glasshouse
A huge conservatory housing a Costa Rican cloud forest and a spiny desert from Madagascar, complete with butterflies and other indigenous animals.

Maltz Museum of Jewish Heritage

The museum is divided into three sections: the permanent exhibits which focus on Cleveland's Jewish community, its history, and its contributions; a portion of the Temple Tifereth-Israel Judaic art collection; and the temporary exhibits, currently home to the "Cradles of Christianity" exhibit.

Cleveland Sports

Then there is Cleveland Sports. In Cleveland, the four recently constructed sports facilities in the downtown are: Progressive Field once known as "The Jake" home of the Major League Baseball Indians; Quicken Loans Arena ("The Q") home of the NBA Cavaliers; First Energy Stadium home of the Cleveland Browns, and the Wolstein Center for the Cleveland State University Vikings basketball team that plays in the MAC Conference and appears off and on in the NCAA basketball tournaments. Each of these venues and teams has their own special nature.

The Brown's who have a storied past in the NFL, but not so much since the name was revived with an expansion team in the 90s, still attract a loyal following that demonstrates a passion for the team and the game, sometimes in bitter winter conditions.

The Indians, who play Major League Baseball have a glorious past, and one of the best settings for baseball in the league, remain another Cleveland team that seems to not be able to get to the pinnacle now without a championship season in a half of a century. Now, they are the team that lost to the Chicago Cubs when they won their first World Series in over a century. But Clevelanders, being Clevelanders do not despair. Their sports glass is always half full. Progressive Field

All one can say about all of these fans and their unrequited passion is this: When (not if) Cleveland enjoys a championship season from these teams, it will generate delirium. Not just joy, not just excitement, not just celebration . . .delirium.

We wrote that back in 2014 when we published our ebook guide on Cleveland. The estimated 1.3 million fans who showed up for the Cavaliers NBA Championship parade in 2016 were just another proof of the prescient nature of our observation, , ,

JACK Casino Cleveland

Located in the historic former Higbee's department store on Public Square in downtown Cleveland.

.

Sporting Events

Cleveland Marathon
Long-distance runners gather from around the globe each spring to Rock 'n Run downtown.

MAC Basketball Championships
The Mid-American Conference of NCAA Division I college basketball holds its annual championship in early March at Quicken Loans Arena ("the Q") to determine a March Madness tournament seed.

Cleveland Outdoors

Lake Erie

Cleveland's inland fresh water sea provides many opportunities for boating, fishing, swimming, and hiking/walking. Sailors, boaters, wave runners, and jet skiers enjoy the lake with marinas, piers, and boat launches available all along America's North Coast. Lake Erie, the shallowest and warmest of the Great Lakes allows for fishing more than three seasons of the year with healthy populations of walleye and perch. In the late fall and early winter, anglers pursue steelhead trout in the many rivers feeding Lake Erie up through Northeast Ohio and into Pennsylvania and Western New York.

Cleveland Metroparks

Ranked among the 10 best big cities for hiking by USA Today, Cleveland's Metroparks form an Emerald Necklace around the metropolitan area, and the miles of paved and unpaved trails encircling Cuyahoga County. The Metroparks easily accommodate biking, horseback riding, jogging, and rollerblading. In the winter, visitors can cross-country ski these same trails.

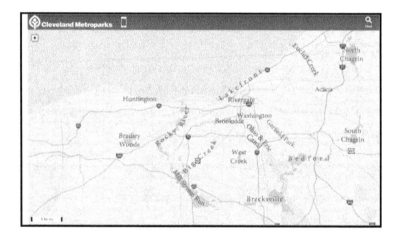

Cuyahoga River

Boaters, rowing crews, canoes, and kayakers enjoy the diverse scenery along the "Crooked River" as named by the Mohawk tribe. The Cuyahoga flows past the nightspots of the Flats (dockage available at restaurants and bars), downtown's towers rising up the hill, active industrial remnants of the birthplace of the petroleum and steel industries, pastoral settings, and the Ohio and Erie Canal.

The Ohio & Erie Canal has been preserved as a core element of Cuyahoga Valley National Park. In Ohio's only National Park, walk or bike the Canal

Towpath. The National Park starts 8 miles south of downtown and stretches for miles down to Akron. The Towpath extends from Lake Erie in Downtown Cleveland through the southern suburbs past Akron, Canton, New Philadelphia, and into rural Bolivar and historic Zoar.

Amusement Parks:

Northeast Ohio offers world-class amusement parks including Cedar Point in Sandusky, an hour's drive west; and Memphis Kiddy Park in Brooklyn, Ohio, a small but fun park for toddlers to pre-teens.

Cleveland Tours

Goodtime III. See Cleveland by water via Lake Erie and/or the Cuyahoga River. Dining and entertainment available.

Nautica Queen. Lakefront and river dining cruises departing from the west bank of the Flats.

Lolly the Trolley. Trolley bus tours offering a variety of routes and lots of information about Cleveland. Tours focus on both history and modern landmarks.

Walking Tours of Cleveland. Various tours, some by foot, others by wheels.

African American Heritage Trail. This tour provides a perspective of the experience and impact of Cleveland's African American community.

Great Lakes Tour Company Cleveland's first bike tour company offers tours of Downtown Cleveland, Ohio City, and University Circle. It also provides bike rentals and free delivery.

Live Music

Cleveland's music scene is an ongoing feast of local, regional, national and international acts that collectively define Cleveland as one of America's Music Towns. We mentioned the world class Cleveland Orchestra, and most of the top touring acts will come to the major venues, such as Quicken Loans Arena.

The superb Blossom Music Center stage in suburban Cleveland has offered great concerts during warm weather months for decades.

Cleveland State University Wolstein Center hosts hip and happening acts as in the kind that appeal to college students.
Cleveland is home to numerous mid and small sized clubs abound around the city.

Cleveland Scene is the local city paper and its website offers an excellent ongoing update on what is happening in Cleveland for all local live music.
The Rock and Roll Hall of Fame brings in live acts that promote and advance their mission. All in all, it is a wealth of music and entertainment

Downtown Cleveland

Obviously, the focal point of Cleveland's resurgance is most evident in Downtown Cleveland. Besides new edifices, more attractions and events for everyone, numerous entertainment districts, and improved transportation choices Downtown Cleveland is now home to thousands of new residents. Indeed, Downtown has become one of Cleveland's largest and fastest growing neighborhoods with verve and excitement available long after the end of business. The main focal points of Central Cleveland are:

Public Square The Civic Monument to the Civil War is the focal point, flanked by Terminal Tower, Jack's Casino, it is the focal point for many of the main streets of Cleveland

Warehouse District The distribution and storage center district for 19th and early 20th century Cleveland is now home to restaurants, nightlife, hotels, and many new residents

The Flats Now being revitalized, this was the original central Cleveland entertainment neighborhood, even when it was a more rough and ready denizens in the days of burning rivers

Playhouse Square Highly respected as one of America's best Theater Districts. It is second only to New York's Lincoln Center in size and scope. Playhouse Square continues to provide top notch live Theater featuring local and nationaly reknowned authors, actors, and creative talent.

Cleveland Playhouse Square
Betwen 13th and 17th Streets along Euclid Avenue

One of the best known Regional venues in America the Cleveland Playhouse is ten venues featuring premier regional theater, dance, comedy and magic performances, music, and teaching the arts and crafts of Theater. Original works first performances has been a hall mark of CPH for over a century. Besides theater and music, back stage tours are available.

The list of theaters include:

Allen Theater
Connor Palace
Hanna Theater
The Helen Rosenfeld Lewis Bialosky Lab Theater
Kennedy's Cabaret
KeyBank State Theater
Ohio Theater
Outcalt Theater, Upper Allen, Westfield, and Studio
Theater

4th St. East The newest of the downtown Enertainment attractions, this robust Restaurant Row incudes restaurants from some of America's most acclimaed Celebrity Chefs, including those from Cleveland.

Gateway

Perhaps the key redevelopment of downtown, this is where the Sports venues for the NBA Cleveland Caveliers, and the Major League Baseball Cleveland Indians stand besides the restaurtants, sports bars, and other destinations who benefit from the throngs who come to downtown to root on their favorite teams.

Cleveland State University: Like any University in a downtown location, the nearby streets are active with students who take advantage of being in a city setting as part of their college experience. Coffee Shops, Healthy Juice bars, and Vegan restaurants stand along side the bars and night spots that cater to University Students.

Lakefront:

Along Lake Erie is where some of Cleveland's most celebrated attractions, including the Rock and Roll Hall of Fame, the Great Lake Science Center, and the home stadium of the NFL Cleveland Browns.

Cleveland Downtown Hotels

Holiday Inn Express Cleveland Downtown
629 Euclid Avenue Cleveland, Ohio
44114

The extraordinary qualities of the Holiday Inn Express start with arrival at the venerable Guardian Bank Building along Cleveland's historic and lively Euclid Avenue, about half way between Terminal Tower and the Theater District. Just a short walk away is popular East 4th Street with its internationally known restaurants and nightspots. Gateway too is short distance from the hotel.

The Guardian Bank Building was at one time one of the tallest buildings in the US. Restored to its original graceful beauty when it first opened as the New England Building in 1894, the experience of staying at the Holiday Inn Express starts with the Corinthian columns that guard the front entrance into the main lobby of marble and granite. The scene is much as it was when this building was a center of commerce in Cleveland.

The welcome stations are just ahead in the grand lobby and the staff is professional and courteous. After a swift check-in, the next place to check out is the guest room.

The guest rooms are superb in many ways, not the least is the use of the existing dimensions of the building re-purposed into spacious and surprisingly light-filled guest rooms. They are the largest standard guest rooms of any hotel in Downtown Cleveland.

Hilton Garden Inn Cleveland Downtown
1100 Carnegie Ave, Cleveland, OH

With one of the best location in the downtown core, the Hilton Garden Inn has easy access to freeways, Gateway and the Stadiums, and the rest of downtown

Cleveland. It also has one of the best combinations of affordability and full service in Downtown. Because it is a Hilton and all that name means for savvy travelers through the centuries the Hilton Garden Inn delivers a higher level of guest service and comfort. Because it is a Garden Inn the setting is more relaxed, business friendly, and most of all, budget friendly.

Because it is so close to both Progressive Field, home of the MLB Indians and Quick Loans Arena, home of the NBA Cavaliers – both in walking distance – The Hilton Garden Inn gets more than its fair share of sports fans, especially those from Indian Nation and Cavs Nation who are in Cleveland to take in a game. That gives the Hilton Garden Inn a special kind of energy when the teams are in town. But they are not always in town, and much of the time the Hilton Garden Inn Cleveland Downtown is busy being a full service hotel with room night prices just about everyone can afford.

Residence Inn Cleveland Downtown
527 Prospect Avenue East
Cleveland, Ohio 44114

What a lot of travelers may not know is that Residence Inns are also a flag that offers some of the most intriguing and beguiling lodging opportunities on the planet. Some are located in the midst of the most celebrated travel destinations on earth. Some of those offer unique settings that go along with a special architectural location. The Residence Inn Cleveland Downtown is one of those places, as it part of one of

Cleveland's restored Nineteenth Century Arcades, right in the heart of Downtown Cleveland.

The Euclid Arcade, the part that houses a section of the Residence Inn Cleveland Downtown is connected to what was The Colonial Hotel on Prospect that is the main tower of the Residence Inn. That makes this Residence Inn one of the largest in total rooms to found in the Midwest. It offers 175 Suites on 7 floors. The suites that are incorporated into the second level of the famed Euclid Arcade open onto the arcade by a hallway so each face the atrium of the arcade. Because it was build to be both bright and inviting it is quite a view. The arcade main floor operates as a retail and business center, and the liveliness of the setting only adds to the Cleveland downtown feel. Across the way from the row of guest suites is the public area where the fabulous complimentary hot and cold breakfast is served, and the flexible meeting space.

Heading to downtown Cleveland for a few days or maybe longer is better staying at the Residence Inn Cleveland Downtown.

Restaurants

Boney Fingers BBQ
401 Euclid Avenue #54, Inside the Historic Cleveland Arcade
Cleveland, OH 44115

Open only a short time, Boney Fingers located on the lower level of the celebrated nineteenth century Cleveland Arcade has already shot to the top of the best places for honest-to-gosh, made the right way, fall apart tender, deep flavored, and nuts good barbecue in Cleveland. Not that Cleveland is that easy of a barbecue town to take by storm. Folks in Cleveland have been slow cooking cheap cuts of meat for way over a century. Perhaps not to the national acclaim of other more celebrated cities, but nothing to sneeze at, either.

That was the discussion when we sat down with two of the family that is Boney Fingers BBQ, Erik and son Christian who along with brother-in-law Paul have brought decades of restaurant industry experience, culinary school training, and home tested tried and true old-timey low and slow barbecue to Cleveland in this wonderful place.

Not much more than a counter and some table and chairs, Boney Fingers is all about getting your fingers on their wondrous meats and chowing down there or take it away for a 'moveable feast' of a kind. They did mention thoughts of a more elaborate place, but if you know barbecue the fancier the place the more in doubt the meat. No doubts about Boney Fingers. This is the bone out best of barbecue, because it is chock full of the one recipe ingredient that the best barbecue must have – time. As Erik pointed out there are no tricks or short cuts to barbecue. The basics are simple: The right cuts of fatty meats, a rub that anyone can mix together, and then an unwavering discipline to cook low and slow and not do nothing to the meat until it is fall apart tender and imbued with all that Smokey flavor.

That's it.

Lord know we tried to coax some other reason or two for why their meats that are getting the local media into such a tizzy – a local media that had a history of uncovering food talents that will go on to become national and international stars. But there was no rocket surgery to uncover. As Erik repeated, ". . do it right and it comes out right." How about that?

Yet, there are some unique things to Boney Fingers that should be mentioned. Not the least of which are the barbecue dishes that we have not seen before. Such as the Philly Cheese Steak inspired CLE. We are always a tad dubious when other classics are 'gussied up' with new fixings, but one taste and the only question is why didn't they do this in Philadelphia first?

Another menu grabber, really isn't a selection. It's a time of day. Breakfast. Boney Fingers barbeque for breakfast. That is deep-down delicious meats that met the low heat in the afternoon of the day before now being dished up with crackin-fresh eggs, crispy potatoes, and even waffles. Yup. Waffles and barbecue. Erik told me the Wrap with choice of meats, stuffed in a spinach tortilla with eggs and browns is the busy Clevelander's dream-come-true. Take that one to work, and the rest of the day is a lark.

Boney Fingers BBQ, morning, noon and night. Just like how long it takes to do it right

The Butcher and the Brewer
2043 E 4th St, Cleveland, OH 44115

There is so much going on at The Butcher and the Brewer; we need to get going right away here.
That is what we learned when we interviewed Jason Workman of the innovative and successful partnership of Cleveland restaurateurs called Cleveland Brewery, Co. They originated the Gastropub scene in Cleveland with their Tremont Tap House. And now they have created a new place in downtown Cleveland that is gaining raves from local and national media.

The main thing we learned is that The Butcher and the Brewer is a lot more than just a first class award winning craft brewery and a superb team of skilled butchers and meat artisans. The Butcher and the Brewer represents a definite approach to animal husbandry that supports local farms and fields and the careful preparation of meats and charcuterie. Then pair these delicious meats with the award winning delicious and exciting craft brews. . . oh my. And in all there is the passion to combine the two in one location along Cleveland's celebrated East 4th Street dining and entertainment destination.

Open only since last year, The Butcher and the Brewer has already become one of the signature location on East 4th Street. That is easy to understand when you enter and see the expansive space with ample communal seating that leads on one side to the gleaming stainless steel vats of the Brewery, and on the other side the display cases that front the working butcher shop where the humanely raised and slaughtered meats are hand cut and processed. And made more flavorful with just so aging and natural flavorings, as in the sausages. The two venerable and ancient culinary disciplines are then combined into plates and libations that elevate each other into a kind of flavor profile Valhalla that has to be enjoyed to appreciate. Their motto sums it up: Old World Cuts and Hand-Built Brews.

And like the best places that emphasize great meats, TB&TB offering of seafood is outstanding. Don't know why this is true, but it is. The choices of Oysters, Scallops, Mussels, Lobster and exceedingly fresh fish team up with the brews as perfectly as the meats.

So, it is not surprising to find at The Butcher and the Brewer genuinely authentic Vegetarian and Vegan selections, as well that belong with great beer. That includes a superb selection of craft made cheeses.

Ranging from light and mild to butter to dense in texture flavor many have re-discovered how cheese loves beer. That romance is on full display at the Butcher and the Brewer.

To call The Butcher and the Brewer a lively place with a high level of guest enjoyment is to be working on a Degree in Understatement. However, finding seating almost all of the time is not a real challenge. It may take a time or two to find one's way through the plethora of choices, but that is duty deemed worthy in so many ways. Groups and Special Occasion folks will be thrilled with the facilities and outstanding food and drink selections, and of course the setting as well. Oh, not to be an afterthought, but The Butcher and the Brewer is a market, too. Take home superb meats, exquisite cheeses, exciting sides and bold brews. Man, what a place.

Lago East Bank
at Aloft Hotel East Bank
1091 W 10th St, Cleveland, OH 44113

Even before the celebrated Aloft Hotel on Cleveland's East Bank was constructed the investors and the flag's parent Starwood Hotels looked for a Cleveland restaurateur with the capability of bringing a destination dining experience for their guests. They wisely chose the Salerno Group; a highly successful family owned and managed company with an established location in Cleveland's Tremont neighborhood. The coincidence that their Tremont place called Lago, Italian for lake, was their perfect choice to be included in a leading edge hotel with stunning views of Great Lake Erie seems inevitable now. That was just one of the insights that Chef Salerno's Business and Life partner Nicole Salerno pointed out as we sat down to learn about Lago, Chef, and their family business successes.

Chef Salerno is highly respected and appreciated in Cleveland, a City that has produced a number of world-class and world-famous chefs. Chef Salerno's passion for beautiful cuisine, served with professional care in stylish and inviting settings was a perfect fit for what is now Lago Cucina Enotecca and Birreria at the Aloft. Along with Mrs. Salerno, Manger Mike Nadolski joined us to impart the full story on Lago. We were charmed by the élan and dedication so evident in the way they describe what Lago is all about.

If there was anything that was emphasized most, it is how Lago like all of the Salerno restaurants are family business where the guests are welcomed with hospitality and sincere deference the same as guests in Salerno home. The same goes for how the staff, from the front of the restaurant to the kitchen are family members. Each hired and trained properly and promoted from within. All the staff and managers take ownership of their part in Lago, and it shows in attention to detail, and pride in their professions.

As much as the service and style are superb, it is Chef Salerno and his accomplished kitchen staff that are stars of the show. The Lago East Bank is about casual and accessible Italian cuisine presented in ways that are both familiar and exciting. Because the restaurant is also the kitchen for the entire hotel, including room service, it is a busy place where the emphasis on fresh ingredients, many from local farms and fields, joins with the Italian passion for cooking that is done just so. This results in delicious dishes in menus from Brunch to late night bites. The choices are not fussy or demanding in any way. They include Italian classics, pizzas, salads, sandwiches, sides and small plates along with new cuisine that brings the best of today's Italy to Lago's tables. Menus include Brunch, Happy Hour, the Main and Lunch menus, the aforementioned Late Night, and Lago Lite. Truly, anytime is precisely the right time to come to Lago.

To fit that level of accessibility and activity, Lago's setting and atmosphere is delightfully accommodating and stylish. The feeling is as casual and inviting as gathering in the home kitchen for an everyone-is-family meal. Whether the occasion is for business, for friends and family to catch-up, before or after the show or game, or just to celebrate the best in Life, Lago of the Great Lake Erie's East Bank is a superb choice.

And, there is the assurance that this family owned and operated business is personally involved in and passionate about the experience of each and every guest. To find that kind of genuine dedication in a family business with the confidence that comes from a well run and managed successful enterprise is rare, to say the least. We are privileged to feature Lago, Chef and Nicole Salerno, and the whole Salerno Group family in our Cleveland City Guide.

The Nauti Mermaid
378 W 6th St Cleveland, OH 44113

Now, when you go you may think that this place has been here since way before the Warehouse District got trendy. And the next nanosecond you are thinking was it always a Key West hangout dragged a thousand plus miles north and dropped in Cleveland? The place where the Nauti Mermaid stands has been in operation for decades. But the NM is more new than that, but the location is decades in the making. It just is too authentic to be otherwise.

The Flats, West Bank

Brick and Barrel
1844 Columbus Rd, Cleveland, OH 44113

Not an expansive Tap Room emporium, Brick and Barrel is more intimate and accessible. Their Brewmaster, besides being a devil with Ales, is also a wine guy, who offers personally selected vintages.

Nautica Queen Cleveland's Dinning Cruise Ship

Sure its on the touristy side, but the social media reviews are decent, and by a water tour is maybe the best way to take Cleveland in.

Gateway and East 4th Street

We are big fans of Restaurant Rows, because they offer great choices in a short distance. Restaurateurs may wish they could isolate their place from everyone else, but that approach is a sure way to go out of business. Even the best out of the way place, like those Provencal French Michelin Guide best are not quite as isolated as a romantic travel writer may want to portray.

So we are delighted to give a head's up on East 4th Street, the narrow in-between street that connects Euclid and Prospect and Gateway which is that part of Downtown Cleveland that abuts Quick Loans Stadium (Cavaliers) and Progressive Field (Indians).

Up and down East 4th are a number of national places, and a couple of local spots, but overall it's the sort of usual collection of Italian, Irish, Sushi-Asian, Gastropub, et with fast turnover, oversize portions, and a predilection to serve alcohol. None of them are really, really bad. So, we are just observing that old Midwestern bromide, 'if you can't say something nice about someone, don't say anything at all."

The street is best known, perhaps, for two places that have obtained a lot of press and media coverage. One is owned by a guy named Michael who has gone from Cleveland to his big time celebrity chef rewards. The other is highly regarded, but consistently gets not so great ratings on the dining apps. The problem with the media darlings are they can garner an attitude that just isn't consistent with Cleveland's authenticity and genuine No BS. So, by all means go and enjoy. But just like the chains, do not make the mistake of seeking out trendy places in Cleveland. That is just an utter waste of a good trip.

Constantino's Markets Downtown
1278 W.9th Street
Cleveland, Ohio 44113216-344-0501

Whether at the Warehouse District location, or the one at Case Western University in the University Circle, Constantino's is a great place to find local, fresh, right beside quick and delicious. Eat at the Café, take out for a delicious picnic, take back to the Hostel for some gourmand home cooking, or cart away for the trip back. Here it is from their website:

A feast for the senses, Constantino's beautifully appointed market welcomes customers with enticing aromas, colorful displays, and friendly staff. In addition to groceries, produce, dairy, fresh meats and seafood, at Constantino's you will also find healthy snacks, organic selections, health and beauty products, gifts, magazines, tobacco, and a wide-ranging beer and beverage selection.

Spend some quality time exploring our oak paneled wine department, which houses an extensive selection of wines, priced from (way) under $10 to Oh Come On. After you've selected some wine, stroll over to our specialty and imported cheese section and pick something wonderful to go with it.

Hungry right now? We've got you covered with our in-house deli, bakery and freshly prepared foods. Our selections range from good old-fashioned comfort food to health conscious to gourmet. Take your choices "to go", or relax in our café. Constantino's Café is a popular gathering place where customers come to enjoy breakfast, lunch, coffee or a snack, and during the warm weather months, outdoor café seating attracts a lively social scene.

Located nearby many of Cleveland's prime attractions, Constantino's Market is the perfect place for a pause before, after or during your sightseeing adventures.

Cleveland East Side

Here are some great places to enjoy, starting in the neighborhood closest to downtown, St.Claire-Superior.

Noble Beast Brewing Company
1470 Lakeside Ave E, Cleveland, OH 44114

Highly regarded Craft Brewery that excels at serving great food with just as great beer.

Slyman's Delicatessen
3106 St. Claire Avenue , Cleveland, OH 44114
(216) 621-3760

If Souza's Marine Band can be called "The President's Own" so can Slyman's be called the Cleveland Deli of the Presidents? Especially those Chief Executives who love to eat really good deli from an authentic legendary Cleveland delicatessen? Indeed, America's last three Presidents have feasted on Slyman's with President George W Bush in person along with the whole Secret Service effect – helicopter overhead. President Bill Clinton and President Obama got their Slyman's, but they had it eating-in when visiting Cleveland; which is the way a lot of people get their Slyman's on.

The crown jewel of Slyman's is the incomparable Corned Beef. They have been preparing the cured beef masterpieces for 60 years. Back since the Slyman family bought the place in 1964.

When we sat down with son Freddie Slyman -- who keeps the family tradition going strong -- he told us that today, as from day one the corned beef is perfectly handcrafted, and then thin sliced to make massive sandwiches that require an unhinged jaw to eat intact.

He also pointed out that Slyman's is a lot more than mind bending Corned Beef sandwiches. Guest feats on turkey, roast beef, pastrami, salami, tuna, ham, egg salad and bbq sandwiches that are just as generous and delicious.

There is breakfast each morning, which is for a lot of Clevelanders how they think of Slyman's corned beef when it is teamed up with fresh eggs, home fries, in hash; even a breakfast sandwich with eggs and cheese.

Freddie wanted us to make this point above all else: Slyman's is about family. It is about the life long hard work commitment his parent's made to do very delicious food right, every day, for decades. It is the way they know their regulars, and love to meet the new folks who come in for the first time. And it is the way they keep up this level of excellence that has spanned millennia. That is why Presidents eat Slyman's. They know Family, America, History, and really good corned beef. That is how you get to be President.

Superior Pho
3030 Superior Avenue E, Cleveland, OH 44114
216.781.7462

Recent online review:
"Don't be deterred by the front of the restaurant. Inside it is clean and has a nice light decor. The pho was hot, the bun was great. The pho broth was not the best though and so I docked a star. I prefer my broth to be darker and more fragrant. Great service, friendly staff more than willing to answer any questions."

Empress Taytu Ethiopian Restaurant
6125 St. Claire Avenue, Cleveland, OH 44103
216.391.9400

Recent online review:
. . . always looking for new things to do and experience in Cleveland. My friends and I spent the evening at the Empress Taytu and I mean the evening. We arrived at 5:00P and left around 8:00P. Definitely plan to spend time and soak up the atmosphere if you like coffee splurge and indulge in the coffee ceremony.

Open Pit Bar-B-Q
12335 St. Claire Avenue, Cleveland, OH 44108
216.851.7709

". . . have been going there since I was about 19 years old I am 43 it is without question my favorite place to eat favorite menu item is there wings with sauce and they are not stingy with the sauce when you ask for sauce on your wings the wing is covered in sauce on a scale 1 to 10 they get a 22."

Goldhorn Brewery
1361 E 55th St, Cleveland, OH 44103

The ample space of Goldhorn's tap room belies the fact that is an intimate space in the sense it is inviting to everyone; from beer fantatics to community folks who like the positive feeling of just being there.

And of course, some really good beer and eats.
Look for their Polka City Pilsner and Dead Man's Curve IPA at local retailers, too.

Agora Theater & Ballroom
5000 Euclid Ave #101, Cleveland, OH 44103

For a city renowned as the home of the Rock and Roll Hall of Fame, one might expect numerous places like the Agora. Well, at least there is the Agora. To be fair, Cleveland has a bunch of live venues. We listed some in the City Guide, as long as they are as interesting and historic as the Agora.

Most shows are all ages. Expect an energetic crowd.

University Circle

The other city center of Cleveland is University Circle. Located a few miles due east of downtown University Circle is easily accessible by car, the Bus Rapid Transportation Health Line, and the Red Line rail makes a stop near Little Italy.

Home to Case Western University, the Cleveland Clinic, and the Cleveland Symphony, University Circle has a world-wide reputation for learning and culture. It is also a beautiful example of the 19th Century Ideal of city spaces, with wide boulevards, civic gardens and parks, museums and stately home among middle class neighborhoods. Any season is a delight to visit University Circle, with Springs and Autumns being especially colorful.

Italian Village is adjacent to the east end of University Circle, and is one of Cleveland's oldest and most intact ethnic neighborhoods. Mostly renowned for block after block of Italian American eateries and shops, the Village is now home to a multi-ethnic neighborhood, including students at Case Western and Health Care workers at the Cleveland Clinic.

Here are a few wonderful places to stay, dine, and enjoy in University Circle and nearby Italian Village

Glidden House
1901 Ford Drive Cleveland, Ohio 44106
866-812-4537

The Gilded Age of the late Nineteenth and early Twentieth Centuries was more like the Roaring Gilded Age in Cleveland. At one point in time Cleveland was home to more Millionaires than any city in America, if not the World. In those days being a Millionaire is a close approximation of being a Billionaire, today.

In the midst of this conspicuous wealth the members of that class included the Glidden Family, namesake and proprietors of the paint company. Anything having to do with construction, from lumber to paint produced vast fortunes as the whole country was on a building binge. The Gliddens did very well.

In keeping with the ways of the culture they participated in a grand home for the Gliddens was a necessity. However, this was not an age given to unthinking excess and nouveau riche improprieties. The model for the wealthy of America was the great of Great Britain with their sense of proportion and unshakable dynasty. The Gliddens built their Cleveland manse true to this ideal. At the Glidden House website there is a full description, here are some excerpts to set the mood:

Listed on the National Register of Historic Places the Glidden House was constructed in 1910 by Francis Kavanaugh and Mary Grasselli Glidden. Their home represents the French Gothic Eclectic style of architecture that was prevalent in this once-prestigious residential section of Cleveland. The design of the mansion was originally conceived by Edward Hughes Glidden and was designed to be the vernacular of the French chateau-style mansions designed during the late 19th century by an architect named Richard Morris Hunt.

In 1953, Western Reserve University (now known as Case Western Reserve University) purchased the house for the Department of Psychology and later it was used for the Law School Annex. In 1987, the University leased the Glidden House to a group of investors who have renovated the mansion to its original splendor.

Mid-Twentieth century the Glidden House was purchased by adjacent Case Western Reserve University. They first used the Glidden House for the Department of Psychology, and then later for the Law School. In 1987 the Glidden Hose was leased to investors who renovated the mansion to its original splendor. During the renovation, great care was taken to restore every detail of the ornate ceiling in the original dining room, library, and foyer. The beamed ceilings in the living room were also uncovered during the restoration process. When viewed closely, the letter "G" appears in the hand-painted filigree of every other beam. The hand carved woodwork was also repaired and restored at the time.

When it was transitioned from university space to lodging, The Glidden House was a bed and breakfast: A large bed and breakfast. It is not that now. The Glidden House is now a Historic Boutique Hotel. The new management, after a meticulous restoration and expansion, now offer the grace and charm of the Glidden House to savvy travelers who appreciate the attention to detail and personalized service that the Glidden House is widely known for. If anything remains from the bed and breakfast past, it is the warm feeling of hearth and home that they offer to guests. Especially with repeat guests, who quickly feel they are part of the Glidden House family. Yet, in every way The Glidden House is full service hotel with all the amenities and services expected.

Finally, the location of the Glidden House is one of its key benefits. The University Circle section of Cleveland is the focal point of the city's world class Universities, Arts, Medical Centers and Attractions. Located east of downtown with easy access to nearby Little Italy and the other revived neighborhoods of East Cleveland, the University Circle area is also known for fine dining, and a lively mix of students, artists, medical professionals, and locals who love living in such an exciting urban environment. Guests will find many wonderful activities and choices just a short walk from the Glidden House. And the new Bus Rapid Transit Health Line, which works like a fast paced street car/bus makes getting back and forth to downtown

Cleveland quick and easy. In fact, Cleveland is one of the few American cities where a train ride from the airport, downtown, and quick access to University Circle are all included for a low cost all day pass.
The Glidden House is beautiful, historic, inviting, and rewarding. Start with a first stay, and you will add it to the list of places to visit every year

Constantino's Market
11473 Euclid Markets
Cleveland, OH. 44106
216.721.6000.

Whether at the Warehouse District location, or the one at Case Western University in the University Circle, Constantinos is a great place to find local, fresh, right beside quick and delicious.

Little Italy

Presti's Bakery and Café
12101 Mayfield Rd Cleveland, OH 44106

Presti's is another one of those family owned Cleveland places that survives for decades and generations on simple greatness. One of the best places to get authentic in Little Italy it is close to University Square, so it should not be missed.

Their website tells the story: In 1903 Rose and Charles Presti Sr. opened Presti's Bakery specializing in baking fresh bread. As the business grew, so did their family and in 1916 Charles Jr. was born. From a young age, he worked at the bakery learning the trade from his parents. The bakery moved locations several times before settling in the heart of Cleveland's Little Italy in 1943.

Charles Jr. married his lovely wife Jean in 1946 and together they raised three children, Charles, Claudia and Sheila. They worked in the bakery for much of their youth, breaking only to attend college. From their parents, they gained the knowledge and experience needed to maintain and grow a successful business.

As the bakery business grew and became more diverse, Claudia and Sheila purchased and renovated the building at 12101 Mayfield Road (the current location) and soon re-opened as Presti's Bakery and Café in1999 with dine-in availability as well as carry out.

At present, Presti's Bakery remains an integral part of Cleveland's Little Italy as well as the surrounding areas, which include University Hospitals, Case Western Reserve University, University Circle and the Cleveland Clinic. Claudia's son Michael is now the pastry chef and fourth generation using only the freshest ingredients to produce the finest quality baked goods. Fresh bread, donuts, cookies, cakes and pastries are still made by hand using the same recipes and techniques originally created by Rose and Charles Presti. The bakery has expanded its menu to include a full line of fresh deli salads, pizza, Stromboli, lunch and dinner specials as well as a catering menu. We look forward to providing you with a "sweet" experience on your next trip to Presti's Bakery in Little Italy.
In the café be sure to enjoy the White Artichoke Pizza, the Pepperoni Roll, any of the deserts, and . . . on a budget? Head over in the morning for the Breakfast Sandwiches, and grab some half priced day-old pastries.

La Dolce Vita 12112 Mayfield Rd
Cleveland, OH 44106

Of the traditional Italian places in Little Italy. La Docle Vita is one of the best. Online reviews rated close to 5 stars after hundreds of reviews. And yes the recipes are time tested and beloved, but the ingredients are always the freshest and finest.

Mama Santa
12301 Mayfield Rd Cleveland, OH 44106

The checkered table cloths, the rewarding Italian traditional dishes, the lively and inviting scene, Mama Santa is that family run Italian place we all think of when we think Italian restaurant.

Its high rating on social media from nearly a 1000 reviews just confirms the obvious.

Angelos Nido Italia Restaurants
12020 Mayfield Rd, Cleveland, OH 44106

Highly regarded Little Italy institution. Social media ratings above 4 ½ stars, from hundreds of reviews. BTW, Angleos may be a venerable place, but it is hardly calcified. Like a family Italian place could be anything but lively? Lively and charming.

Etna
11919 Mayfield Rd, Cleveland, OH 44106

Intimate, with one of the nicest outdoor spaces in Cleveland, Etna is also a highly rated Little Italy restaurant after over 200 online reviews.

Etna stands out too because its menu hews toward contemporary Italian cuisine. Not that there is anything wrong with the traditional Italian American dishes, just it's nice to enjoy more Italian Italian when in Little Italy.

West Cleveland to Lakewood, Ohio

From here on out, we traverse the western parts of Cleveland out to nearby Lakewood. We start in Ohio City and Tremont, the other parts of Cleveland that had experienced a remarkable turn-around. Ohio City, as the name implies was once its own municipality before being absorbed by growing Cleveland. Ohio City and its citizens continued to retain their identity as a special part of Cleveland though good times and bad. It is the home of one America's best City Farmer Markets, the West Side Market and now one of the best Craft Brewery scenes in America.

Ohio City

West Side Market
1979 W 25th St. Cleveland, Ohio 4411321

Northeast corner of Lorain Ave and W 25th St. Located near the Hope Memorial (Lorain-Carnegie) Bridge, this Old World produce market across the Cuyahoga River from downtown in Ohio City offers an arcade area containing shops with food of Irish, German, Slovenians, Italian, Greek, Polish, Russian, and Middle Eastern descents, among others. Its origins date back to 1840 making the West Side Market is Cleveland's oldest publicly owned market and one of the oldest in America.

The centerpiece of the market, the yellow brick market house with an interior concourse, was designed by the architects Benjamin Hubbel and W. Dominick Benes who also designed other famous buildings in Cleveland, such the Cleveland Museum of Art.

New West Side Market House, Cleveland, Ohio.

Last year it is estimated that over a million people visited the market. Whether as a day-tour destination or a weekly shopping experience, the West Side Market continues to be an interesting and historical Cleveland tradition.

Hostel

The Cleveland Hostel
2090 W.25th Street Cleveland, OH 44113
216.394.0616

Cleveland Hostel is easily the largest and most modern hostel in the Midwest. Opening just a short time ago, this large hostel offers over 10,000 square feet of newly renovated accommodations right in the heart of Cleveland's Ohio City just steps from the West Side Market, the Red Line RTA train, and all the happenings on West 25th Street

It is the hard work and inspiration of owner Mark Raymond, a native from Ohio's Northeast. As their website notes:
As a four year old Mark was intrigued with Cleveland and its skyline; when asked in preschool what he is thankful for, Mark replied, "The Terminal Tower."

Mark's fascination with all things urban continued as he pursued degrees in urban planning and traveled to more than 70 countries staying in over 100 hostels worldwide. Mark saw a need for a hostel in the city he loves and is thrilled to offer travelers, volunteers, and sightseers on a budget, clean, affordable and social accommodations.

Their website goes on to note:
Cleveland Hostel is a Modern American Hostel of over 10,000 square feet. We offer both shared and private rooms with a total of sixty beds. All of the bathrooms

are individual with a shower, sink, and commode and are only a few steps away from the sleeping rooms. Some of the private rooms have an attached bathroom. We have wonderful common spaces where travelers can mingle with others guests. We have a spacious and fully equipped kitchen and dining room so you have a place to prepare and enjoy the treasures of the West Side Market. Relax in our two comfortable lounges as well as the rooftop deck with fabulous views of the Cleveland skyline! We invite you to take advantage of our convenient amenities such as bike rental and storage, free wifi, and free parking across the street.

We are located in the heart of the great Ohio City Neighborhood. In less than five minutes walk you can be at the amazing West Side Market, many unique shops, fantastic dining, and many bars and breweries. In just a couple minutes you can also walk to the RTA Red Line Train to destinations such as Downtown, University Circle, the airport, and to eight more bus lines. Use the Ohio City W/25th St. Train Station and the West Side Market bus stop to reach the hostel. RTA bus and train schedules are on Google Maps, it is the best way to find your way!

When we stayed at the Cleveland Hostel we were impressed with how it has all the best hostel features: kitchen and laundry facilities, locker space, comfy sleeping spaces, inviting communal areas, and more.

What sets Cleveland Hostel apart is just how well planned and high quality everything is inside and out. The kitchen is a great cooking space on its own, and could easily accommodate a good-sized get together. The rooms, both bunks and individual are unusually spacious for a hostel, newly decorated and comfy. The lockers are big and well positioned. The access is easy and secure. And even though the Cleveland Hostel is located on West 25th just across the Hope Bridge from downtown Cleveland is it a quiet place in a great urban setting.

If you are thinking that a hostel is a cramped place where the price makes the experience okay, Cleveland Hostel is roomy, new, safe, smart and low price: One of the best in the country.

Campbell's Sweets Factory
2084 W 25th St, Cleveland, OH 44113

Steps from the Hostel is a home for sweet things, made there and made fresh. Not just buckeyes and cupcakes, Campbell's is primarily celebrated for their fresh popped popcorn. Flavors run the gamut from sweet to salty to savory. Great place to visit first to grab something to munch while taking in Ohio City, or last on the way back the Hostel to share.

Craft Beer and Restaurants

Bookhouse Brewing
1526 W 25th St, Cleveland, OH 44113

A Nineteenth century brewery building returns to its first purpose now with books, creative and delicious craft beers, dogs and cats, ciders, tin ceilings, open mics, pop-up gourmet eats, and special events. A neighborhood gem. Not much has changed.

Market Garden Brewery and Distillery
1947 West 25th Street
Cleveland, Ohio 44113

Starting off the remarkable restaurants, breweries, distilleries and convivial destinations of the Ohio City Market Garden group is the Market Garden Brewery and Distillery. Indeed it may be one of their newest locations, but in many ways it is the epitome of their dedication and passion for great brews, spirits, food and time.

Our visit with Sam McNulty, one of the Ohio City partners and a driving force let us get a picture of how they made all this happen and where it is going.

Sam is a bone-out Cleveland guy, from Cleveland Heights. He got into restaurants when we went to Cleveland State and opened his first restaurant on the Cleveland State campus in his junior year. Wisely they had 6 beers on draft, and 5 were local craft beers: Great Lakes, Burning River, Western Reserve, and more. Insight is where most successful business starts from and Sam and his partners have proven to have insight by the barrel.

Sam got his degree at CSU, in urban planning. This set the stage for all that the Market Garden Group has done in Ohio City. Ohio City itself was not a neglected Cleveland neighborhood per se. It already had the vaunted Great Lakes Brewing as a not-so-long-ago arrival and the venerable West Side Market since the turn-of-the-century. So, for Clevelanders and visitors Ohio City was not some undiscovered gem. It was however, woefully under-appreciated and developed.

 Through the turn of this century Ohio City seemed stuck in limbo while other neighborhood like nearby Tremont were catching a wave. The main drag was doomed, it seem to be permanently dowdy and funky with little charm. When Sam and his team help kick-start start this recent reincarnation they may not have seen it as a grander plan of urban renewal. After all it was more than enough to just want to sell, then make, great beer and the right cuisine that goes with it. But, in a short amount of time, the bigger picture thing came along. Soon the starter place – Bier Market, came with the next door place: The Bar Centro. Then there was the Speakeasy, and viola one side of 25th around the corner from Great Lakes is one of the best beer destinations in America.

Cross the street and just down from the West Side Market Sam and them got a fabulous space for the Market Garden. Expansive, in a Midwestern way, it offers ample room for the world-class brewery; new distillery; eats, events, music, special occasions, and Sam's favorite – Author Readings. We love all craft breweries. They have transformed American taste for beer back to the venerable past of true brewing Art. But we especially love how at the Market Garden Brewery is great brewing, distilling and a cultural resource, and there is just no other way to put it.

Okay, Beer.

Think of the best of European styles done to a tee for American love of variety. Ales, sure: Brown, Scotch, IPA and Pale – some of the best in America. Lagers? Absolutely. Market Garden has the facilities to make lager in proper temperatures, including Pilsner so crisp, clean and flavorful. The British family of Bitters, Porters, and Stout are permanent residents. Over from Bier Garten are their first love and greatest accomplishments: The Belgium Beers including Wit and a superb collaboration with their neighbors at Great Lake. Seasonal beers such as Bock are not only reason for repeated excursions. In just about every way you can think of it for the beer aficionado, or just beer enjoyment Market Garden gets it all right,

Food: Great cooking that uses beer and is for eating with beer is the total experience at Market Garden.

Two things stand out. Some are the vegetarian choices that pop-up throughout the menu. Beer does not need meat to be enjoyed – obviously. So no meat and healthier fare are amply available at The Market Garden. The other are the reasonable prices for great food. This is Cleveland, after all, and guests do not pay a premium, or expect to pay a premium for simply choosing a great, popular place to eat and drink. That dog don't hunt in Cleveland.

Beer should be enjoyed any day, at any time. It is liquid bread. One of the best weekly occasions at Market Garden is the Brunch. Sunday from 10 AM to properly late as 3 PM, the brunch menu gives guests choices that go with beer and then some. There are eggs as omelets and deviled; waffles, pancakes, beignets, pierogies and more.

Bier Markt
1948 West 25th Street Cleveland, Ohio 44113

McNulty's Bier Markt has been Ohio's only Belgian bier bar since opening in 2005, serving over 100 Belgian and American craft beers along with over 30 rotating drafts. Nestled in the heart of the historic Ohio City Entertainment District with over two dozen bars and restaurants in the surrounding blocks, the Bier Markt has the taken the lead in changing the beer culture and bar experience in Cleveland.

Since opening Bier Markt a new level of beer appreciation and understanding has blossomed in Ohio City. Because they offered over 100 Belgian and American beers it was a fast study in what makes both extraordinary.

Right along Bier Markt couples the great beer from Belgium and America with dishes that are equally delicious. Because Belgium beer offers so many flavor profiles, and aspires to a fineness in taste and aroma, the food side can be that much more expansive . . .

Bar Cento
1948 West 25th Street Cleveland, Ohio 44113

So, along comes Bar Centro, a Modern Italian Eatery. At Bar Centro the menu items do change over time, and freshest and finest along with local dictate some of the availability of any dish. Nonetheless guests will find menu items that reveal the best of the Belgium and American Craft Beers when paired with this great food.

They say:
Bar Cento, located in historic Ohio City, offers a creative European-inspired menu that focuses on regional and sustainable ingredients sourced from local farms and purveyors. The cuisine is served with a rustic presentation inside the sophisticated yet comfortable dining room, accented with haute-bucolic décor and a sixteen-seat bar built using wood from a reclaimed Amish barn. Our award winning seasonal menu is complimented by an extensive and carefully prepared wine list. Bar Cento, recently touted as having the best pizza in Ohio by Food Network, serves food till 2am every day of the year. Come check out one of the premier dining destinations in Cleveland.

Speakeasy
1948 West 25th Street Cleveland, Ohio 44113

Okay, you went across 25th from Market Garden and you dropped in at Bier Markt. Ate at Bar Centro. Drank some more there, too. Now you can go downstairs to the Speakeasy for delicious, special cocktails.

Nano Brew
1947 W 25th St, Cleveland Ohio 44113

When you take into account the general philosophy of the Market Garden group;
Namely great beer, food, and civic revitalization than Nano Brew are another happening place.

So, the beers will change with seasons, and styles but be assured that superb Nano and Market Garden brews are featured along some of the best Craft Brews from no further than across the street at Great Lakes and as far away as Akron.

Here Brew Master Andy Tveekrem brings over two decade of award-winning brewing experience to this small but mighty brew house to turn out adventurous and at times experimental brews. Andy is an Ohio guy, and this is where he displays the best of his impressive beer know-how.

They say:

Bringing The Craft Of The Brew To Lovely Ohio City. Nano Brew Cleveland is a friendly neighborhood brewpub with 24 beers on draft both at the inside bar and at the lively outdoor Beer Garden Bar. Enjoy a freshly brewed beer from our 1 barrel brewhouse or any of the other local craft breweries we feature on draft. Brewmaster Andy Tveekrem brings over two decade of award-winning brewing experience to this small but mighty brewhouse to turn out adventurous and at times experimental brews. From one of a kind brews to recipes that might make it to full scale production at our Market Garden Brewery & Distillery just down the block, the lineup of beers will change daily.

We love to ride bicycles almost as much as we love to drink beer with family and friends, so we decided to collaborate with our neighbors Joy Machines Bike Shop on the Nano Brew Bike Tune-up Station inside the bar. All the bike tools you'll need to get your two-wheeled steed back on the road are free to all. And there's a drink rail to rest your brew while you work on your bicycle. Did we mention that your bike helmet gets you half-off your first beer? There's nothing like the old "brain bucket" to keep us safe while we enjoy cruising on our bicycles.

Our fun and simple food menu is sourced from local and often organic farmers and butchers. The free-range Ohio Beef burger patties are hand ground daily by Vince Bertononaschi at the historic West Side Market just down the block. Our fruits and vegetables come seasonally from local farmers including the Refugee Response volunteers at Ohio City Farm across the street from us.

So, we started with beer and end with Bikes. Not really the end, though. When we met with Sam he let us exciting possibilities that will only improve Ohio City, Cleveland, and the enjoyment of everyone who wants to drink and eat well.

ABC The Tavern
1872 W 25th St, Cleveland, OH 44113

The atmosphere is Cleveland originals meet Millennial and Zs looking for the Authentic. That, and lower-side prices for really good food and fun drinks keeps ABC hopping.

SOHO Chicken + Whiskey
1889 West 25th St. Cleveland, OH 44113

SOHO, as in SOuthern HOspitality ,is Cleveland's Ohio City best place to eat, drink and slow down, Southern Style. The owners Nolan Konkoski and partner Molly Smith are two young Cleveland culinary professionals who bring years of experience running the front and back at some of the Cleveland's best places. Now, at a perfect spot on Ohio City's West 25th street they have put their talents and insights to work giving Cleveland a place that is Southern based in style but all North Coast in effort and execution.

At SOHO that means the grits are made to perfection with corn meal from the Southern icon Anson Mills. It means the greens are bursting with flavor and never overcooked. It means the Duck Gumbo is drop dead good, made with chicken, shrimp, andouille, Carolina gold rice, field peas, Cajun pork rinds and rich duck confit,

Naturally we have to note of the true-to-the-south Southern Fried Chicken, that is the highlight of the entrée menu. It is hard to imagine a chicken dish that has more permutations in taste and texture than Southern Fried Chicken. For most folks their only acquaintance with the real thing is by inference, as it comes from the kitchens of Yankees, without much true knowledge of how it should look and taste. At

SOHO it is real Southern Fried Chicken. Crispy, juicy, bursting with flavor – a savory delight that seems more like a confection than a main meal. They spend a lot of time and effort to do their chicken right at SOHO.

This wondrous Southern Fried Chicken can be enjoyed, in a fashion, morning, noon and night. The entrée selections say as much because they offer Chicken and Waffles as the Mornin' Style; with mashed potatoes and country gravy as the Evenin' Style, and with baked macaroni and cheese for the late night repast.

In each instance the Fried Chicken is king, but the sides and the way they are made take it to that proverbial higher level. Such as the Waffles that accompany the Fried Chicken are crispy rosemary waffles served with bourbon-spiked Ohio maple syrup. It may be Southern, but this Chicken and Waffles has got an Ohio thing going on.

The Black Pig
1865 West 25th Street, Cleveland, OH.
216-872-7551

French inspired and local fresh and best is a combination that garners a lot of praise from the attuned locals who are being spoiled rotten by so much great food and drink. French inspired for classic preparation and presentation, but not goofy French. This is beer and spirits food. Burgers, Schnitzel, Chicken, Pork Tenderloin and House Sausage line up with hearty Steak Frittes, Roasted Duck Breast and Viet-Franco Bahn Mi sandwiches. (Vegetarian or Pork and Chicken pate with Pork Belly) French flair and confidence is evident in dish after dish. At the same time, Clevelanders who expect and get to eat hearty no-fooling-around food come away satisfied. Even when they are tucking into a Croque Madame made with Ham, Gruyere, Mornay, Egg and grabbing a craft brew to wash it down.

Nonetheless, French inspired is not French indeed unless it comes with some great wine choices. The Black Pig steps up with Red, White, and Rose/Sparkling/Desert pours that offer delightful choices from France, the rest of Europe, North and South America. Without any possible feeling of inadequacy, guests happily ask the knowledgeable staff to recommend matches to the dish. It's the kind of place that gets the whole wine and French thing right: Good, never intimidating.

Finally The Black Pig is about local source farms and purveyors. So close to the venerable and vital West Side Market, Chef has taken advantage to pursue his own belief that local fresh is the best of the best in so many ways. That is why the name is indicative of this approach, being that Chef has sourced local heritage swine such as large black hogs for this restaurant trade right along.

Included in the list of local farms and farm products include: KJ Greens in Ashtabula, Refugee Response Farm across the street from the restaurant, Tea Hills Pork Farm in Loudonville, and Rittman Orchards in Doylestown.

Oh, and in the same vain, check out the cool murals of that cover the interior walls by local artist Bob Peck.

The Art of cooking, imbibing, keeping it local, and on the Walls is what The Black Pig is all about.

Flying Fig
2523 Market Avenue
Cleveland, Ohio 44113
216-241-4243

This is where Chef Karen Smalls comes in. Partly by choice and somewhat by chance, Chef Smalls put into practice her firm beliefs that the best comes from local farms. To do this was not just a matter of heading out and getting it. She immersed herself in the local agriculture of Northern Ohio, one of the most diverse and abundant growing areas in America. It has been since the Erie Canal connected the Midwest farms to the markets of New York and beyond. Besides the expected grain and cornfields, Ohio is ideal for growing just about every vegetable one can think of. Then there are fruits that do so well close to the moderating climate of Lake Erie, such as berries and grapes. The Northeast Ohio Vines that have been a part of an active viticulture for centuries. And tree fruits, as well. Add in the outstanding animal husbandry that includes the Amish farms near Canton and New Philadelphia, and it is easy to see how Chef Smalls was able to match invention and inventory.

That is what the Flying Fig is all about, and has been since the last century. Starting with its proximity to Cleveland's landmark West Side Market, and just across the street from the celebrated Great Lake Brewing, the Flying Fig has become as much a landmark with grateful Clevelanders as any restaurant in this hot restaurant town.

When you go to Flying Fig, you are going to find out how creativity and locally sourced really do produce tastes and aromas that are unmatched.

At this point in describing less committed restaurants, we could go through a litany of menu choices to describe the approach and results of the creative minds behind the menu. At Flying Fig, the menu combines readily recognizable classic American dishes. When we were there, Karen was offering Chicken Meatballs made with her particular flair plated with Yukon Mashers and local Arugula pesto.

And the Hamburger is made with local Miller Farms grass-fed beef, along with bacon, Prairie Breeze (locally sourced) Cheddar and fries. From this solid base, Karen branches out to dishes such as Roasted Local Winter Squash Quinoa made with apple, mushrooms, leeks, herbs, feta, greens, toasted walnuts and Poblano-maple butter. Another dish we encountered was the Grilled New Creations Pork Chop with a smoked onion Bourbon reduction and cheesy grits and caramelized Brussels sprouts.

Because it was winter, many of the dishes were hearty. The Seafood Stew made with the Fish of the Day is more than satisfying even though the scallops, wild shrimp, mussels, and Basmati rice are enlivened with a coconut-curry broth. But not all the dishes at Flying Fig are big eaters. The many small plate selections display Karen's skill and creativity, again featuring the best of farm to table.

A tribute to the nearby West Side Market was The Market at the Fig Cheese Plate includes Jasper Hills Farms Bayley Hazen Bleu, Tarentaise, apples, walnuts, date-port chutney, and honey crostini: A small plate serving, but no less satisfying.

Expect the menu to change with the seasons, availability, and opportunities. With her insight and contacts, Karen is one of the first to know when something exciting is happening with the local farmers.

Duck Island

No ducks. No island. What gives?
Ah, but it was a good place for rum runners and
bootleggers to seemingly disappear when the Feds
and Revenuers were getting too close for comfort
back in the heydays of Prohibition in Cleveland.

And the locals were more than happy to keep things
flowing along, with nary a thing to say about the
goings on. One of those many places in the U.S. where
Prohibition was just a nasty rumor.

Velvet Tango Room
2095 Columbus Rd Cleveland, Ohio 44113

In keeping with the uninterrupted history of adult
beverages in Duck Island is one of the best Cocktail
Lounges in the U.S.

Classy, smart, intimate, and always fascinating the Velvet Tango Room offers creative and classic cocktails and libations matched with gourmet small plates, and of course, Jazz. Though there is not a strict dress code, please know one will feel like a fish out of water popping in with baggies and flops. And who doesn't deserve an evening out with adult ladies and gents, delicious drinks and food, and virtuoso Jazz? Looking dapper and smart is a small price to pay.

Forest City Brewery
2135 Columbus Rd, Cleveland, OH 44113

A few doors down from the panache and posh of the Velvet Tango Room is one of Cleveland's most comfy and casual Tap Rooms. The rich history of Duck Island and Cleveland beer brewing are the backdrop, but the attraction is some of the best craft beer in town. All matched with meats, cheeses, pretzels and breads – heck you can bring in your own grub to eat with their great beers. That's jake with them.

No wonder whiling away the days and evenings are just something that happens at Forest City.

Tremont

Tremont is one of the original, if not the original Artist Pioneered revitalized neighborhood in Cleveland. The closeness to downtown, the potential charm of the housing, and its low cost drew in Artists and then the restaurants and shops that followed. Indeed, enough of these Artists accumulated in Tremont that something of a Tremont School of Art was recognized. Though the housing costs have risen by at least double, a lot of the original vibe of the artist colony remains. Hope that it lasts a long time.

Prosperity Social Club
1109 Starkweather Ave
(216) 937-1938

We get such a kick from the Prosperity Social Club. Wow! What a place. It's a time capsule. It's a lively neighborhood magnet. It's a first class drinking and eating place with an authentic retro reality. It's that place where having a good time is all you want to do as soon a you walk in, and they are there to help.

There is Bonnie and her team of cooking, serving, and pouring stars. Bonnie comes over to Tremont from years of experience running some of the best places in Cleveland. Along the way she finds this long time social club on the southern side of Lincoln Park on Starkweather in Cleveland's Tremont neighborhood. Bonnie knows the history of Tremont and knew that the scene was about artistic cool and Cleveland real. So, just getting the space that is the Social Club set the stage for bringing together great food and drink in a place that cannot be anything else but inviting. As they put it on their nifty website:

When we talked with Bonnie it was just before the evening rush on a late winter's evening, and the warmth inside made the compelling case for stopping in at Prosperity. Nonetheless she got us the story of how this place was even more than a dream come true. On sight she knew how she was going to keep the place as real as it seems, and yet get it in line with the wonderful things happening now in the Cleveland going-out scene. That includes the antique bowling machine, pool table and wall games. Music and events are a part of the Prosperity too, with Old World (Polish) Wednesday featuring the appropriate music (Polka) and warm weather Two Wheel Round Up for pedal, motorized and monster sized vehicle with two wheels, or so.

Food at the Prosperity Social Club is in keeping with its setting and neighborhood. We like the way they keep it within reason including price wise. So they usual expectations of sandwiches, burgers, Cleveland standards, steaks, chicken and seafood are all there, but many times they get a kick start to greatness. Hence, you can get Pork Loin and Pork Empanadas. Panko is the dredge for the fresh oysters and the coating with herb on the Tilapia. The Cabbage Rolls are Hungarian style with a Paprikash sauce. Chicken Soft Tacos with cilantro-lime jicima slaw; Potato Pancakes with Apple Chutney; Mac and Cheese on shells with a slew of choices to make it a meal.

Speaking of good times, the drinking choices for those who choose adult beverages is rewarding but never over-wrought. On draft are local and national craft beers and overseas favorites. In cans and bottles are even more choices along the same lines, and some brands that seem to be pulled out of a time machine cooler in the back. When I was there a Balantine Ale in the iconic can canonized in bronze by Jasper Johns was enjoyed with the Potato Pancakes and apple chutney. Gosh, it was good.

Naturally there are selections for those who eschew alcohol. Also, do bring the kids. The Prosperity is a neighborhood place, and families do feel right at home getting something to eat whether they live around the corner, or are from the other side of the globe.

Part of the fun with kids, those who can, are the aforementioned heritage games that are a part of the Prosperity vibe. Even the decor festooned with period neon, and brick-a-brac from the Brewer's promotions of the time is something all ages enjoy. Lastly, Bonnie ask us to remind folks that intimate gatherings, corporate functions, and special occasions are something that are done at Prosperity with aplomb.

Civilization
2366 W 11th St, Cleveland, OH 44113

Just on the other side of Lincoln Park from Prosperity is the Termont neighborhood coffee place in a 19th century abode with that special, authentic feel that the usual spare and plastic coffee dive doesn't have.

You could say it is on the funky side – like that is an issue in Cleveland? – but regardless its consistent high social media ratings bespeaks of just how, well yes, civilized Civilization truly is. Wouldn't know it?

Tremont Tap House
2572 Scranton Rd, Cleveland, OH 44113
216.298.4451

Right at the beginnings of the Cleveland Craft Brew
scene, and indeed in those Halcyon days of Tremont's
emergence as an Artist's haven, The Tremont Tap
House began pouring superb brews, serving delicious
food, and creating the kind of neighborhood
destination that endues to today. It is hard to imagine
the Tremont turn-around happening without the
Tremont Tap House. Just as it is with the wave of
Cleveland Craft Brewers who depended on the
Tremont Tap House to showcase their beers and ales.
We were reminded of all this when we interviewed
Jason Workman, one of the working partners of
Cleveland Brewing Co, home of Tremont Tap House
and the fabulous The Butcher and the Brewer on
Cleveland's East 4th Street happening.

Right from the beginning and true to the whole idea of a gastropub, the Tap House boasted a meticulous and extensive selection of hand crafted American and European Beers. Today's list has more than 100 examples of fine beer, with about half on tap. And, as all great gastropubs do, the expansive list of beers matches brilliantly with the unexceptional fare conjured by the magicians of the culinary team.

Though the wizards of the kitchen have changed over the years – indeed as Jason told us, many going on to start their own landmark places, making the Tremont Tap House as much as incubator for Cleveland's celebrated dining scene as it is for the landslide of great breweries – the absolute dedication to freshest and finest with an emphasis on locally grown and raised became the hallmark of the Tremont Tap House. And it set the stage for the extraordinary things happening at the The Butcher and Brewer.

When you visit the Historical Italianate on Scranton Street with its blend of contemporary and industrial design, it is the warm and inviting ambiance that gets your first attention. It is easy to understand how the Tap House became such an important gathering place for the Tremonters who fell in love with this wonderful Cleveland neighborhood. Many of those folks are artists, and adjacent to the 40-foot concrete bar are four distinctive booths each crafted by a local artist. That is not to leave an impression that the Tap House is a stuffy place. Just the opposite. With 8 large HD TVs to keep up with the glorious exploits of Cleveland Sports teams, and a 2000 square foot outdoor patio that comfortably seats 50 shows the Tap House is a lively and happening place. Many of the best parties and get togethers take place at The Tremont Tap House. The open kitchen highlights the dining room, while their lounge offers a more intimate and easy going feel.

As for the beer and the food. Suffice to say those items change with some predictable regularity, true to the philosophy of freshest, finest and local. Nonetheless, in true Gastropub style the emphasis is on appetizers, sandwiches, burgers, pizzas, and salads mainly with an entrée menu that is just as outstanding. And the Tap House was one of the first places to get into Sunday Brunch and show that the neighborhood beer and grub place was the perfect spot for a Sunday repast to enjoy and relax.

As well conceived and manage as the Tremont Tap House is, Jason told us that they were looking for the right place to take their insights and knowledge base to a higher level of accomplishment. That place is the new place on Cleveland's restaurant and entertainment attraction, East 4th Street. Called The Butcher and the Brewer it is also featured in this City Guide in our section on downtown Cleveland.

Fat Cats
2061 West 10th Street Cleveland, OH 44113

The neighborhood place is what our guides are really all about. We try our level best to just avoid places that are ubiquitous, or want to be. We want to tour those places that ring true of the street, neighborhood and city where they belong.

Then there are those places that make the neighborhood. The place that comes along as the neighborhood is coming to life. That is Fat Cats.

When Tremont was a rumor among Cleveland Artists that cheap rents and cheap space butts up against the Cuyahoga and downtown were there to be had, Fat Cats was up and running.

When top national publications for the gourmand take note of Fat Cats being one of the Nation's best of its kind, then someone(s) is doing something right. Those someones now are Chef Ricardo and he told us that the menu is always changing. Fat Cats commitment to fresh local and seasonal best requires an expansive repertoire of cooking know how. Chef puts his well-honed execution along with the rest of the team to work every day meeting that ideal. And the results show.

Starting to sound like Fat Cats is for, well Fat Cats, uh? Ooops. Do not get that idea. Fat Cats is not a fancy way to eliminate the kids college fund in a night or two. Just the opposite, Clevelanders demand you feed them and not leave them penniless. Fat Cats is for clever diners who know how to eat really well, for a little scratch.

The nationally known Fat Cats was called by Bon Apetit magazine one of the best neighborhood restaurants in the country. Fat Cats offers a stunning view of downtown Cleveland. In the summer there is the patio for outdoor dining. Throughout Fat Cats are paintings by featured local artists.

They serve lunch, dinner and weekend brunch. Friday they keep the kitchen running until Midnight. A great spot for a late repast on a wild Cleveland night where the view is just intoxicating. Yeah, you read that right – Cleveland.

And great for kids and families and those just knocking about on a superb Cleveland Day. The charm of Fat Cats starts when you approach the neighborhood house and storefront. It fits right in with the Tremont scene. Well it should. Pretty much got that whole thing going two decades ago.

Lucky's Café
777 Starkweather Avenue Cleveland, OH 44113
216.622.7773

For Tremont, and Cleveland Lucky's Café is a gem of a bakery and café that serves superb breads, deserts, confections along with the best breakfasts and lunches. The ambiance is pure, authentic Cleveland.

Lucky's Café is a touchstone place in the ongoing movement that is often called Fresh Local. Way before this exciting way of bringing the best to the table was being adopted by National chains and Big Restaurant corporations, Lucky's Café, and more to the point, Lucky's Café Master Baker and Culinary Revolutionary Heather Haviland was proving that Fresh Local not only can work, but that it is superior to any other way of provisioning and preparing crafted foods.

We had the privilege of sitting down with Heather on a beautiful, warm Summer day at Lucky's garden, when she had some time after the morning baking and before the lunch rush. The garden was lush with many of the fresh vegetables, fruits, and herbs that are destined as ingredients for Heather's Art.

The story of Heather is story of a young Chef who used her talent and dedication to great cooking as a personal life adventure. Starting from her home in Buffalo, she wended her way to the West and back again, always expanding her knowledge and skills with the mentoring help of equally dedicated professionals who saw in her their own passion for great cooking and baking.

That is what she is saying in the mission statement that is located on Lucky's website:

To provide the people of our community
with pastry and breads which are made by hand
with care and attention to quality,
using only the freshest of ingredients.

We support and promote our Ohio farmers and producers
by showcasing the bounty of their harvest in our products.

We offer our customers an alternative to the mass produced
by committing our passion for the craft to creating good wholesome food.
We will remain creative with and inspired by the cultural diversity and layers of tradition our community offers to everyone.

At Lucky's the whole experience is an urban delight. The venerable structure that is Lucky's occupies a stretch of Starkweather in Cleveland's Tremont that is both neighborhood and creative inspiration. The interior is intimate, and inviting with a rustic feel that cannot be made without time's passage.

Lucky's Café is what happens when a passionate, dedicated culinary genius puts her love of food into the context of what is best for all of us, and our planet. It is just one place, but Lucky's is one place where the best of fresh, local and sustainable is made with creativity and insight. Thanks, Heather and your talented crew.

Dante's Tremont
2247 Professor Avenue Cleveland, OH 44113
216.274.1200

In the Renaissance that is the Cleveland restaurant scene, Dante Boccuzzi stands out as one of the most successful and acclaimed Chef/Owners on the North Coast. He has obtained this level of accomplishment by executing his intense knowledge of cuisines and restaurant management with precision and aplomb. Anyone who knows anything about the Restaurant business knows that having success and then duplicating that success without giving up the bedrock integrity of skill and taste is almost impossible. To do so with a timeless sense of grace and balance is even harder to comprehend. But, that is what Chef Dante Boccuzzi has managed to do for years, and the accolades of his guests are the living proof of this.

At his signature restaurant in Tremont, Dante's we had a chance to chat with Chef Boccuzzi and talk about the philosophy of his cuisine, or should we say cuisines, and how that guides the restaurants of his group.

Because his passion for great food, wine and spirits has taken him to so many places on this planet, Chef has been able to glean from his wide breadth of knowledge elements of world cuisines that lend themselves to each other. This, along with his inestimable understanding of individual styles and techniques is the palette he creates his own creations from.

Chef's training in classic and modern Japanese cuisine is on display at Ginko. It is generally considered one of the best Japanese dining experiences in North America. The full retinues of Sushi, Nigri, Otsukuri are served. The creativity at Dante's is evident in the Omakase menu choices where the Chefs present only the most stunning fresh choices with classic Japanese perfection. Again, the menu selections are augmented by a superior choice of Asian and non-Asian libations. Their Happy Hour, may be the freshest and most flavorful in Cleveland

Barrios Tremont
806 Literary Rd, Cleveland, OH 44113
Phone:(216) 999-7714

Great Beer and Spirits, delicious inexpensive tacos, late night Cleveland: We can pretty much stop right here, because that is just about all those in the know need to read.

Barrios has a lot more than just those three unbeatable elements, but it always seems to come back to the fact that in a town that prizes a high level of conviviality, Barrios gets that passion for fun just right.

When we sat down with the General Manager it was at the cusp of another day and night of Barrios in Tremont. Ahead lay the serving of a lot of world-class beer and whiskey and tacos made right now from delicious meats and fillings, with the best tortillas in Ohio, all at the guest's directions.

It goes on like this for a taco eternity. And at a few dollars a pop, the chances to imbibe ones fancy is not hampered by ready funds.

Now all this fine noshing is a good thing, but at Barrios the tacos are made to enjoy with outstanding craft beer and premium spirits.

They also have a nice selection of good wines and by the glass for easy enjoyment. The Sangria is made with authenticity and flair.

Now, we have gone on a bit after a simple first sentence we described as saying it all about Barrios. So, it is evident there was more to say. Even more is that there are mutilple locations. The one in Cleveland's Tremont neighborhood that is fast becoming an icon in a neighborhood that is a Mecca for some of the best dining and imbibing in the US. The other is not far to the West in Lakewood, and it to is a Cleveland, or Greater Cleveland favorite.

Sokolowski's University Inn
1201 University Rd. Tremont - Cleveland, OH 44113

We are featuring some of the oldest places in Cleveland in this ebook, and well we should. They are time tested for decades and offer authentic good times that never go out of style. Perhaps the most emblematic of this extraordinary class of classics is Sokolowski University Inn in Cleveland's Tremont. The University Inn's (on University Road) name does actually have some connection to higher learning, in a most round about way. Tremont was platted to be a College Town. A long since un-realized institution was to occupy the area and hence it is noted that many of the streets feature names that would be in keeping with its scholastic purpose. So you see street names: College, Professor, Library, and our favorite Literary in Tremont. University was perhaps the highest aspiration of the developers naming tendencies. No University of Tremont. No College, either. A University Inn? You bet your dupa!

And since 1923. The host of Millionaires that called Cleveland home was at their zenith. The City was at its zenith. Building monumental bridges across the Cuyahoga river flats. So a bar close to the Iron Workers in Cleveland's Southside (later called Tremont) was a smart move. A smart move made by a Polish-American family, the Solowoski. Now, three generations later the triad that runs the place – Mike, Bernie, and Mary Lou – are keeping a good thing going in much the way it has always been, with a hat tip now and then to current trends and favorites that add some variety. Not that much of that is ever needed. The basics, the Polish American cooking, beers and sprits and enough camaraderie to start an

Old World Revolution, are always there and going strong. The Pirogies get national attention, the Kielbasie is genuine and served right, and don't forget to try the piggies (cabbage rolls). But, the University Inn is a Great Lakes Midwestern place. That means they feature Salisbury Steak, Beer Battered Lake Perch, Breaded Pork Chops, Meatloaf, Walleye, and those never-fail ethnic favorites Bratwurst, Chicken Paprikash, and Eggplant Parmesan.

Finally a word about the lively scene at Sokolowski"s. Local music legend Tom "Mr. T at the Keys" Ballog is at the keyboard playing Wednesday through Saturday hours. Because the University Inn attracts as diverse a crowd as they come – from young to old; terminally hip to babushka mamas; it is good idea to check in on the wait. Though, any wait is worth it.

Hotz Cafe
2529 West 10th Street Cleveland, OH 44113
216-771-7004

Our tour of the best of multi-generational owned early twentieth century Cleveland heritage drinking and eating establishments continues at Hotz Café located on the eastern side of Tremont proper. (Proper? Tremont?)

The Hotz Café is where the same family for 4 generations, the Hotz has served the high and mighty but mostly the local and lucky their favorite ice-cold beer or adult beverage and genuinely delicious food.

Here are some of facts and insights they convey on their website:
The Hotz's Cafe is located in the Tremont area just outside of downtown Cleveland. Opened in 1919, the bar has been in the Hotz family for four generations. There is history galore in the building and if the walls could only talk, they'd have many a tale to tell.
Hotz's Cafe is a traditional "old style" tavern with a friendly staff and regulars both old and new! Whether you arrive in style or with soot all over your face, it makes no difference at this tavern. The patrons are friendly, the food is delicious, and the beer is cold and cheep. What more could you ask for?

On their history:
Where good friends meet" has been the motto of
Hotz Café in Cleveland's Tremont neighborhood since
John Hotzs grandfather bought and opened the café
in February 1919. John Hotz became the third
generation of his family to run the little neighborhood
bar, when he took it over in 1997.

It not only drew the local railroad and steel workers, but celebrities like Ty Cobb, Babe Ruth, Lou Gehrig, Franklin D. Roosevelt, Rocky Colavito and various prize fighters and others through the years. "Babe Ruth came in here and bought a round for everyone. He wrote out a check," John Hotz said. "My grandfather said that was one check he would never cash. We still have it."

Andrew J. Hotz Sr., John's father, took over the tavern and ran it for 50 years. He ran a "tight ship" and didn't allow any problems to even materialize inside, John said. That was well documented when some of the cast and crew of the 1978 movie "The Deer Hunter" stopped by Hotz Cafe. Various Tremont locations were used in the film. "Robert DeNiro, Meryl Streep and others from the movie stopped in here one day after filming," Hotz said. "My dad refused to serve them. He told them to take it somewhere else "My dad threw out Robert De Niro and Meryl Streep!"

Ready-to-bake pizzas are available for those who want the taste of freshly baked pizza in the comfort of their own kitchen.

West Side of Cleveland

Heading west from Ohio City and Tremont are numberous great places to enjoy on the way to Lakewood. Here are a few we recommend.

The Harp
4408 Detroit Ave, Cleveland, OH

Though we put The Harp in among the Ohio City locations it is more a part of the greater West Side geography located on wide Detroit Avenue where it skirts Lake Erie just west of downtown. In fact, The Harp is almost in a place unto itself where the only scenic elements are the Lake and the busy road. Such is the setting for a great place that is perfect for a few hours of splendid sustenance and relaxation.

When we sat down with the ownership at The Harp we quickly learned that it was the culmination of an American Irish families dream to have an authentic but American place for enjoying the Irish Pub. As general contractors they conceived The Harp in how the building would be designed and constructed. All based on first hand knowledge of the Pubs in the Old Country. So, the familiar looks of warm woods and an expansive bar are there. At the same time the picture windows that overlook Lake Erie add a modern sense of space and season. Not many Irish Pubs that incorporate the views of a vast fresh water inland sea.

Starting with this amalgamation of the authentic and modern, The Harp adheres to the same when it comes to food and drink. As much as Americans struggle to understand the inseparableness of cooking and cork the Irish have no such dichotomy. Good food and fine libations should always be a day's reward. At The Harp they are for lunch, dinner, and into the wee hours.

On the Irish side are a collection of Boxty Cakes for lunch and dinner that offer a gourmet appreciation of the traditional Irish potato pancake. In short order the selection include Salmon, Steak, Chicken, Corned Beef, Turkey Reuben, and Vegetarian. In each case the perfectly crispy Irish potato favorite is folded over and stuffed with the featured meat or vegetables and delicious stuff. Yes, its Irish alright, but it today's Irish style of the gastropub.

Along with the Boxty Cakes, The Harp also offers Irish traditionals like beer batter Fish and Chips and Shepard's Pie. But, that is just a smidgen of the menu. Included are Cleveland Slavic favorites such a pierogies both for dinner when served with a creamy Lobster sauce, and as an appetizer from Ohio City featuring Yukon Gold potatoes, white truffle, Fontina cheese, and rosemary topped with caramelized onions and chive sour cream. Goodness. Then Italian inspired dishes and Greek inspired dishes, and a host of delicious choices that make up The Harp's inspired menu

And other cuisines are not just limited to Cleveland heritage. How about Humus appetizers, and Thai Vegetable Stir fry? And authentic Italian: Oh yeah. But Northern Ohio inspirations is found in the Ohio Maple Walnut Salmon, where rich salmon filets are sautéed with authentic Northern Ohio Maple syrup for a glaze and served with candied walnuts and Yukon Gold mashed potatoes.

No Irish place worth it's salt is going to skimp on libations. At The Harp the best of Irish brew are proudly poured. Of course Guinness Stout, Harp Larger, and Smithwick's Ale on draught constitute the Irish imports.

As good as all that is, be sure to check out the menu of half/half pours. As close as beer comes to the blenders Art, these delicious combinations include the celebrates Black and Tan with Bass and Guinness, and Black Velvet combining Guinness and Angry Orchard into a smooth delight.

Irish Whiskeys and premium spirits are served, many in intriguing cocktails that show the international flavor of today's first class Irish Pub.

When the weather's good in Cleveland along the lake, The Harp has some of the nicest outdoor seating one can imagine for any Irish Pub. The landscape that includes shore side industry just seems to fit the whole vibe to a tee.

Old Fashion Hot Dogs
4008 Lorain Ave, Cleveland, OH 44113
(216) 631-4460

When Emanouel "Mike" Vasilou opened a hot dog shop on Lorain, Frank Roosevelt was thinking about Alfred E Smith's wanting him to run for Governor of New York. Talkies were a novel way to watch a movie but just a fad, and Cleveland was still whirling in the Roaring Twenties. In the decades that followed, Mike's Old Fashion Hot Dogs became one of those venerable places of American urban legend where the city's best days, and worst days were celebrated and endured by a parade of citizens ranging from the everyday folks and campaigning politicians, to slumming nouveau riche, and the transient famous all trooping through Old Fashion Hot Dogs.

Okay, there must be one of these places in every American City of any size, and as in Cleveland more than one if you count Steve's Lunch just up the road on Lorain. They all share a funky charm, often ensconced in a small space with a patina of authenticity mostly from not being updated, ever. They are all precious, and in an age of world-wide fast food franchise lowest common denominators they are the actual proof of the idea that a fast delicious lunch served with friendly care and special ingredients is one of the pinnacles of civilization.

What sets Old Fashion apart from all the others is the food. No, not the hot dog. As is the case in so many of these kinds of places, the hot dog is good, but not especially so. It is all that stuff that surround the tube steak that make a 'hot dog' the nifty and venerated dish in the Vahalla of the low end eating. At Mike's that food that defines their Old Fashion Hot Dogs is the chili.

The combination of chili and hot dog seems to more of a Midwestern presentation than anywhere else. In just a few hundred miles from the banks of the Ohio in Cincinnati to the shores of Lake Erie in Cleveland and on to Detroit and Flint chili on a hot dog is de rigueur. Most often defined by the word 'Coney' the combination of hot dog and chili seems at first notice an unnecessary intrusion of one great dish upon another. Perhaps, but not without a happy result. In the case of the venerated use of Cincinnati Chili on a hot dog the practice takes on its own legendary status. Though to the most of us Cinci Chili is that foundation ingredient in a compilation dish that can scale to the heights of '5 Ways" (Cinci chili, spaghetti, shredded cheddar cheese, beans, and diced onions) for Cincinnatians the preferred eating pleasure in on a shortened soft bun with and equal length wiener topped with Cinci Chili and mounds of mild cheddar cheese. The truncated size demands to be served in six-pack denominations.

Chili from Cincinnati is the starting point that takes the Tex-Mex meat and chili sauce dish for a long journey to the Mediterranean when Greek Immigrants arrive in the booming Midwest and take up restaurants as a way to survive and thrive. Their own ancient cuisine is imbued with subtle insights into the way spices and herbs elevate the coarse and cheap into the sublime. Chili was ideal for this kind of improvisation and soon enough Nutmeg, All Spice, Cinnamon, Cardamom and Turmeric were swimming in a Bowl of Red.

So was tomato. In Cinci recipes of any authenticity tomato is a key ingredient adding rich sweetness and piquant acidity, as per the Tex-Mex version,

So, when you sit down to an Old Fashion Hot Dog ladled with their long simmering chili, or a bowl on its own, you get the rich color, meaty fullness and imponderable spicing that any Cinci Chili lover may recognize. What you do not get is tomato. None. That is one of the reasons why Old Fashion Hot Dog chili is a thing unto itself. It may be the indescribable combination of spices and herbs (they will never tell) as well, but your best clue is the lack of tomato. Some kind of ancient alchemy is afoot. Indeed, online sources note that the original-original chili – the mole from Mezzo-America kitchens was sans tomato. So, two ancient worlds agree, chili, yes, tomato, no.

Now add in that this secret recipe has lasted in one extended family for nigh on a century and you will be even more impressed. In a day and age when secrets are anything but and that email you sent to your girl/boy friend to tell them you are having second thoughts is still a cause for mirthful quotations at the NSA; to have a secret like the Old Fashion Hot Dog chili recipe survive, intact and beyond deciphering is something the old heads at the CIA should study and emulate.

Finally are the nice people who run Old Fashion Hot Dogs. These ladies are of Mike's extended family and came into ownership of the joint decades ago. This means that the secret has held firm no matter what, and the not-so-secret sterling service and superb cooking go on. Go to Old Fashion Hot Dog and do yourself a favor.

Bike Shop

Fridrich Bicycle
3800 Loraine Avenue Cleveland, Ohio 44113
216.651.3800

Fridrich's is practically an institution in Cleveland.
They started out as a coal and feed store back in 1883,
and moved across the street to their current location,
in Ohio City, in the 1890's. Since then, they have
expanded to become one of the oldest and
largest bike shops in the U.S.A.!

Gordon Square Arts District

Just west of Ohio City along Detroit Avenue is the Gordon Square Arts District. It is a catalyst for a compelling combination of housing, new businesses, neighborhood beautification, and of course, the Arts. Though Gordon Square is a City planned result of the restorative power of Arts and Creativity in an urban setting, it shares much in common with the more organic creative neighborhoods such as Tremont and Ohio City. It resonates with the same verve and vitality, and offers the visitor numerous opportunities to be entertained and rejoice.

Gordon Square Arts District is helping to infuse more than $500 million in economic development in the surrounding community. This is one of the most substantial commitments of resources to an Arts District in America.

The foundation of the Gordon Square Arts District is a triad of established and successful arts and non-profit organizations that provide unique entertainment, attracting audiences from throughout the region. Already the success of Gordon Square is attracting interest from urban advocates from across the nation, and even internationally.

The Capitol Theater
1930 W. 65th Street, Cleveland Ohio 44102
(216) 651-7295

The Capitol Theater is one of the most exciting places for moviegoers in Cleveland. Operated in the way of the repertory cinemas that were once widespread in major urban centers, the Capitol Theater offers a year-round selection of independent, foreign, and documentary films – many which have limited theater releases in the US.

However, unlike the Spartan confines of the cinemas of the past, the Capitol is a renovated classic neighborhood movie house built in 1921 that offers guests an expanded lounge and concessions including beer and wine. Amid the walls decorated with murals and the classically inspired architecture are the latest amenities of the 21st century cinema including digital project and 3D capabilities.

Cleveland Public Theater
6415 Detroit Avenue, Cleveland Ohio 44102
216.631-2727

The largest of the Cleveland Public Theaters, including
a storefront theater and other performance spaces,
the Cleveland Public Theater in Gordon Square offers
theatrical performances that span the Arts.

Musicians and performance artists work to create a universe of creative enterprise through the seasons at CPT. The CPT emphasizes plays by local and national playwrights along with touring companies with performances that challenge and entertain the savvy theater public of Cleveland and Northeast Ohio. Gordon Square is also home to the Near West Theater, and they have some big plans coming soon.

Gypsy Beans & Bakery
806 6425 Detroit Avenue Cleveland, OH 44102
216.939.9009

In Gordon Square, on Cleveland's West Side is a coffee and bakery place that is pretty much exactly what you think every honest-to-gosh local, community oriented, globally responsible, creative, friendly, indispensable neighborhood coffee and bakery place should be. All that is because the good people who own Gypsy Beans and work there are fans of that kind of coffee bistro, and decided in order to have one, you have to do one.

The Gypsy part of the name is in honor of the
Nomadic people who proudly carry the name, and
how their travels resemble the journey of the coffee
bean from its origins as a libation in East Africa, to the
Mediterranean Basin and the Near East, and then to
Europe where it was embraced as much more than an
uplifting hot beverage to become an important part of
Culture. Along the journey of the coffee bean it has
always been prized for its special ability to enhance
the time people spend together with the rewards of
flavor and stimulation. Though the coffee has been

the focus of any number of kinds of establishments, from a humble purveyor pouring a cup to travelers, to elaborate coffee housed where the business of empires and kings was discussed and gossiped about for centuries.

In this country coffee has always had its place, from the salon to the chuck wagon. Then, in the late 20th century it seemed to be reborn, or at least redistributed out of the kitchen and restaurant coffee shop, and back into the coffee houses where the emphasis was on the brewed roasted bean, and all it can offer. In the midst of this coffee house revolution it became apparent that the whole business of coffee was replete with the problems that plague the Third World, where so much of coffee is grown along the Equatorial latitudes. In good time numerous, and many unsung coffee importers, roasters, and purveyors demanded that the way the coffee is grown and harvested is just as important as how it is prepared. They set a stage for a new appreciation of the grower and the workers who toil to provide, not just coffee, but all manor of agriculture's bounty. Add to this list Gypsy Bean & Bakery where they pay close attention to how and where their beans are grown and by whom, so that in every way they can they can assure their guests that they are the last participants in an enterprise that values human beings and the environment.

Enough of the big picture, let's get back to the delicious small stuff.

Not only a coffee house, and not least of which, Gypsy is a bakery too. A bakery that is both in service of the coffee and teas but is a stand-alone delight.

And Gypsy is a mid-day bistro. Their website captures this well:

The Gypsy's Bistro Menu is gathering of recipes and ideas from experiences wandering the world. The menu changes weekly and we use only the freshest seasonal ingredients available. Start traveling through your day with such delights as a Stuffed Croissant, a slice of Quiche or Strata.

So when you are in Cleveland's West Side anywhere near Gordon Square, stop wandering and head to Gypsy Beans and Bakery.

Toast
1365 West 65th Street Cleveland, OH 44102
216.862.8974

When we sat down with the owner Jill Davis told us that Toast is not just a restaurant per se, but is the end point of a process of finding and supplying the best of Farm to Table. And not just in the nearby farms and fields, but even across the street where they have their own city garden. It was putting those pieces together, plus relying on the insight of like-minded restaurant owners such as Chef Karen Small as Flying Fig (also featured in this travel guide ebook) that gave her the guidance to be this successful, this soon. That, and the food is really good, the service is outstanding, the atmosphere is delightful, and wine list is superb. Of course, all of that is easier said than done.

The reason guests come back time and again to Toast, and have made it a neighborhood favorite in just a short while, is the way the fresh/local sourced ingredients are combined with an intriguing and accessible wine list -- that is one of the best in town. At its heart, Toast is a wine orientated place with an inviting bar that overlooks the big street-side picture windows. It is one of those places where it is perfectly all right to come in and have a glass of delicious wine, a few small plates and perhaps linger awhile. Then, if so inclined, pick up your glass and proceed to a table to order an exquisite dinner and perhaps end the evening with Chef's sweet tooth favorite, or a beautifully crafted cocktail.

On the menu that kind of conviviality is manifest in many ways. The menu is described on social sites, like *Yelp,* as small plates and tapas, but that is way off the mark. The list of menu choices is streamlined to reflect their interest in fresh from the farm and field, and it certainly offers much more than light bites in between sips and gulps.

Toast is gained the kind of reputation that other places only garner after years of trial and error. That is always going to be a tribute to the hard work and dedication of Jill and her marvelous staff. Add in their commitment to the best that local providers can achieve and helping them sustain and thrive—well there is only one thing to do—raise a glass to Toast.

Terrestrial Brewing Company
7524 Father Frascati, Cleveland, OH 44102

Located up along the Lake Erie shore, this handsome brewery tap room has gained an excellent reputation for tasty craft beers and its large, welcoming setting.

Lakewood Ohio

A charming close by suburb of Cleveland, Lakewood is attracting new residents who want to enjoy its nearby location and swell combination of zero lot line businesses, tree lined streets and easy access to downtown Cleveland.

Distill Table
14221 Madison Ave, Lakewood, OH 44107

Locally source organic ingredients are distilled by Distill Table at their local facility and then served with creativity at their full service restaurant and bar.

The restaurant too is dedicated to fresh and eco-sustainable cuisines from the kitchen of Chef Eddie Tancredi. Adding to the warm feeling inside is the Communal table. Indeed the whole place is communal friendly.

Buckeye Beer Engine
15315 Madison Avenue Lakewood, Ohio 44107
216-226-BEER

What better way to start a trip west to east in Cleveland than getting beer and grub at the legendary Buckeye Brewery's own Buckeye Beer Engine? Actually located in the next town to the west along the banks of Lake Erie, Lakewood Ohio, the Buckeye Beer Engine is the place where the decades of craft and skill demonstrated by Buckeye Brewery meet the dishes and delights that they know work best with great beer. So, the menu is how burgers, sandwiches, and flavorsome appetizers go with beer. And not just Buckeye's legendary brews, but many of the best beers that are being brewed across the country.

A lot has been said and written about the accomplishments of Ohio and Midwest Craft brewers in the past few years. And some of the newbies are accomplished Masters in their own right. But in Ohio, Buckeye Brewery and brew master Garin Wright have weathered the storms, sailed the seas, and shown the way going back the century before. For the beer aficionados that may be reading this, a visit to the Beer Engine (and if you are an aficionado, we do not have to tell you about Beer Engines) is all the reason there need be to visit Lakewood, Ohio.

Griffin Cider House and Gin Bar
12401 Madison Ave, Lakewood, OH 44107

If your familiar with these British traditions of craft
cider and gin making then you know that the two are
all that better when offered in one place. That and the
attention to detail that goes into the brewing the cider
and mixing of the gin cocktails has pulled Griffin to
the near top of positive social media ratings from
hundreds of enthusiastic reviewers. Most say it is the
Best Gin House in the Midwest AND the Best Cider
place in the Midwest. All of this without a hint of
pretension or guile. So Cleveland. . .

In conclusion:
We want to underline that this ebook is not intended to be an all-encompassing guide to this great city and its environs. This is a visit guide. The visit can be short, or long, or in between. It can be anytime of year and it can naturally be one of many. And most important of all, this visit guide is a starting point. It is suppose to give a visitor a good start in Cleveland. Enjoy.